Showtime!
Worship in the Age of Show Business

by
Dan Chambers

Copyright ©1997 by 21st Century Christian, 2809 Granny White Pike, Nashville, TN 37204.

ISBN# 0-89098-155-8

Earth in fact does hold treasures,
and it is to those treasures that I dedicate this book
with undying love and devotion

My wife Leola,
my daughter Andrea,
and my son Chris

Table of Contents

* For use as a 13-week study, I recommend combining two of these chapters to make one lesson.

Preface

The church doesn't exist in a vacuum. It exists in a context. It exists in a culture. Consequently, the church will naturally reflect in some ways the culture in which it exists. But to what extent should the church reflect its culture? To what extent should culture influence and shape the church—her beliefs and her practices?

One of the most visible and controversial ways that modern American culture is currently influencing the church is in the area of public worship. Determined to be "culturally relevant," more and more churches are reshaping their public services to include show business elements.

Should the church simply hand over public worship to the show business demands of our age? Or are there valid reasons to protest against pouring public worship into such a format? This book is designed to help those struggling with these questions.

This study has three parts: (1) it examines and evaluates the reshaping of public worship which seems to be epidemic among American churches, (2) it examines and evaluates four trends which some are aggressively promoting in the public services of our fellowship, and (3) it attempts to set forth a biblical "theology of worship" and offers practical suggestions for "improving" our periods of public worship.

It is my prayer that this study is not only well thought out and sound biblically, but that it is presented charitably and with respect toward those with whom I may disagree concerning some matters which pertain to public worship.

With Appreciation

My most sincere and warmest thanks to:

Dr. Harvey Floyd—for prompting me to think deeply about what it really means to worship God; for encouraging me to tackle this difficult topic as a master's thesis; for chairing my thesis committee; for promoting the publication of this material; and for inspiring me to love Bible study.

Dr. Marlin Connelly and Dr. Rodney Cloud—for taking time out of your extremely busy schedules to serve on my thesis committee; for your constructive comments; and for your brotherly support.

Dr. LaGard Smith—for reviewing my manuscript with such professional strictness; for challenging me to think through many things more carefully and thoroughly than I had ever thought before; for your constructive comments, keen insights, sometimes brutal honesty, and helpful suggestions.

Section One
Contemporary Worship

Chapter 1
Bored to Tears

To say that modern worshipers are generally bored with traditional public worship would be to state the obvious. Informal polls and formal studies alike consistently confirm this. For instance, Andrew Hill of Wheaton College reports that for years he has surveyed his students on a variety of topics including worship. The question he asks regarding worship is framed something like this: "How would you describe the worship experience in your home church?" He states that, "invariably and now predictably, the majority of students answering summarize their experience in one six-letter word beginning with b—'Boring!'"[1] Similarly, one of the authors of a recent study which examined the increasingly popular practice of "denomination switching" said that modern worshipers are not leaving churches because they are angry, but for a variety of reasons, one of which is "they're bored by it."[2]

With shouts of "boring," many modern worshipers are demanding that churches refashion public worship or else. The "or else" is usually unstated, but almost always implied, and generally means "or else we'll take our attendance and contribution and leave." A recent newspaper article illustrated this point when it reported that a large evangelical church lost hundreds of members "over disagreements with that church's leaders" regarding, among other things, "worship style." Not surprisingly, it reported that tensions were "drawn roughly along generational lines." The conflict "culminated in a walkout of many younger families" after a congregational vote clearly showed support for the preacher.[3]

Why Are We So Bored?

Why are so many modern worshipers bored with traditional public worship? Before answering this question it is important to understand what I mean by the term "traditional worship." Most would probably agree that, in part, "traditional worship" refers to a service which utilizes the same basic format which churches have used for centuries. What is that format?

For one thing, traditional services are largely dominated by verbal discourse. At a time when many churches are trying to increase the visual stimulation of their services by adopting features like dramatic productions and dance, traditional services still opt for the centuries-old arrangement of one man standing in front of the congregation reading Scripture or expounding it in a lecture format.

A second characteristic of a traditional worship format—at least in most churches of Christ—is congregational singing. In our fellowship, those who would adopt the use of soloists, quartets, choirs, and other types of "special" music would certainly be considered non-traditional.

In addition to being characterized by a particular format, traditional services, as most would also probably agree, are characterized by a particular style. And like the format, the style is one which has characterized most public worship assemblies for centuries.

Perhaps nothing reflects a traditional style quite like the music of a service. Songs in a traditional service are generally characterized by reverent, majestic melodies. Modern music with driving beats and pulsating rhythms are seldom heard in traditional worship services.

A second style characteristic of a traditional service is that its mood and tempo are not always "upbeat"—sometimes they are, but not always. Sometimes the mood and tempo of a traditional service may be characterized as solemn, or even somber—it all depends on what is being discussed and meditated upon at any particular moment during the service. In stark contrast to this, it seems that many churches today are minimizing the use of anything that may slow the tempo or drag the mood of a service down.

As far as style is concerned, perhaps there is one other characteristic of many traditional services that should be mentioned. At a time when many churches are working hard to create a more relaxed, informal, or casual atmosphere for public worship, traditional services often maintain a more formal ambiance. What do I mean by formal? A formal atmosphere for worship is one where the service has been carefully planned and executed, and every aspect of it is carried out with great dignity. Also, one would rarely find anyone serving publicly at many traditional services dressed casually, and the movement of the attendants could almost always be described as "stately."

I would emphasize, however, that this level of formality is not characteristic of all traditional services. I am personally acquainted with many congregations which utilize both a traditional format and style, yet no one would dare describe the atmosphere of their services as "stately." I might add that in some of these congregations there is hardly a tie to be found, even around the necks of those leading the singing, voicing the prayers, or passing the communion trays.

Now that we have a basic understanding of what I mean by "traditional worship," let's return to the question, "Why are so many modern worshipers bored with traditional public worship?" Quite frankly, some are bored because the public services of some congregations seem to be little more than cold, uninspired ritual. I am convinced, however, that many more are bored because one of their primary goals in worship is to get a personal payoff which traditional services simply are not designed to provide.

What exactly do they want from worship? The answer to this question, in part, lies in their complaint that traditional services are boring. "It's boring!" means "It's not emotionally stimulating!" Therefore, when it comes to public worship, it seems clear that a primary goal of many modern worshipers is to have an emotionally stimulating experience.

We should also note that this quest for emotional stimulation in worship is often masked, even from the worshiper himself, by the seemingly worthy goal of "experiencing" God or "feeling" close to Him. For instance, one newspaper article recently reported that many "baby boomers" are returning to "church life" after long absences. The partial reason one woman cited for her return was, "what I decided I needed in a church was a spiritual *experience* at worship and communion. . . . (emphasis added)."[4] It would seem fair to say that by a "spiritual experience" she meant an "emotionally stimulating" experience.

Emotional stimulation, however, is only part of the answer to the question, "What do modern worshipers want from worship?" The full answer is discovered when we understand that, among the modern generation, emotional stimulation is almost inseparably tied to entertainment. In other words, as far as the modern generation is concerned, emotional stimulation and entertainment are two sides of the same coin. Therefore, the full answer to the question, "What do many modern worshipers want from worship?" is "They want to be emotionally stimulated through entertainment."

Another way of saying all of this is to state that having fun and feeling good are primary goals of many modern worshipers. One preacher recently suggested this when he urged churches of Christ to make their services more exciting. He was quoted as saying, "Many have left looking for the experiential aspect of religion . . . Baby Boomers' lives are so filled with worry about economics and relationships that *they want a place where they can flat out have some fun* (emphasis added)."[5]

When having fun and feeling good are primary goals in worship, it is easy to understand why most would find traditional services boring. While traditional services can be emotionally inspiring or stimulating, they really are not designed to be entertaining. In other words, the elements or format of traditional services simply do not have a very high "entertainment value." While worshipers may have fun in traditional services—if they do, well and good—these services are largely designed to teach worshipers Christian truth and the proper applications of those truths (1 Corinthians. 14:26).

Why This Goal?

Why is the achievement of fun and a good feeling a primary goal of many modern worshipers? I believe one major reason is that they have not been taught what it really means to worship God. I believe another major reason is that they are addicted to entertainment (entertainment produces emotional stimulation). In all fairness to the modern generation, however, they must not be held totally responsible for this addiction. They just happen to have been born and reared in a society that is overly-stimulated through constant exposure to entertainment.

Before moving on, perhaps it would be beneficial, or at least interesting, to consider just how such a society may have developed. Although many factors no doubt contributed to its development, Neil Postman, a professor of communication arts and sciences at New York University, persuasively argues that television is largely the culprit. He is quick to point out, however, that it is not the technology of television itself that is chiefly responsible, but rather America's unique use of it.

Unlike many other nations, American television employs a medium of entertainment for virtually all of its programming, or as Postman says, "entertainment is the supraideology of all discourse on television."[6] He continues, "No matter what is depicted or from what point of view, the overarching presumption is that it is there for our amusement and pleasure."[7] The phrase "serious television," he contends, "is a contradiction in terms" for it "speaks in only one persistent voice—the voice of entertainment."[8] Postman observes,

> American television is, indeed, a beautiful spectacle, a visual delight, pouring forth thousands of images on any given day . . . television offers viewers a variety of subject matter, requires minimal skills to operate, and *is largely aimed at emotional gratification.* . . . Even commercials, which some regard as an annoyance, are exquisitely crafted, always pleasing to the eye and accompanied by exciting music. . . . American television, in other words, is *devoted entirely to supplying its audience with entertainment* (emphasis added).[9]

Even worship has not been spared from being presented as entertainment on American television. Postman titled an entire chapter of his book "Shuffle Off to Bethlehem" to illustrate this point. He reported that he watched forty-two hours of "television's version of religion" to prepare himself for writing the chapter. Here is his conclusion:

> Forty-two hours were entirely unnecessary. Five would have provided me with all the conclusions, of which there are two, that are fairly to be drawn. The first is that on television, religion, like everything else, is presented, quite simply and without apology, as an entertainment. Everything that makes religion an historic, profound and sacred human activity is stripped away; there is no ritual, no dogma, no tradition, no theology, and above all, no sense of spiritual transcendence. . . . [10]

By making "entertainment itself the natural format for the representation of all experience,"[11] American television has helped create a society which believes entertainment is the model for properly staging the world. As a result, virtually every aspect of American culture is now dominated by entertainment. Postman notes:

> It is not merely that on the television screen entertainment is the metaphor for all discourse. It is that off the screen the same metaphor prevails. As typography once dictated the style of conducting politics, religion, business, education, law, and other important social matters, television now takes command. In courtrooms, classrooms, operating rooms, board rooms, churches and even airplanes, Americans no longer talk to each other, they entertain each other. They do not exchange ideas; they exchange images. They do not argue with propositions; they argue with good looks, celebrities and commercials. For the message of television as a metaphor is not only that all the world is a stage but that the stage is located in Las Vegas, Nevada.[12]

Perhaps nothing more clearly reflects the dominance of entertainment in American culture than the fact that entertainment is becoming the primary means of engaging the interest and attention of modern students at every age and grade level. As Postman observes,

> teachers, from primary grades through college, are increasing the visual stimulation of their lessons; are reducing the amount of exposition their students must cope with; are relying less on reading and writing assignments; and are reluctantly concluding that the principal means by which student interest may be engaged is entertainment.[13]

Postman's observation was recently illustrated on a network television news story about one school system's attempt to teach young people financial skills. It reported that teachers were sent to a conference to learn how to make the material "fun" for their students.[14] Similar examples could be cited almost to the point of disgust.

Historically, the foundation of this overly-stimulated society was poured more than a century ago. Postman notes that for two centuries public discourse in America was dominated by a thoughtful exchange of ideas through print and verbal means. He terms it the "Age of Exposition" and says exposition is "a mode of thought, a method of learning, and a means of expression."[15] He observes:

> For two centuries, America declared its intentions, expressed its ideology, designed its laws, sold its products, created its literature and addressed its deities with black squiggles on white paper. It did its talking in typography, . . . which has the strongest possible bias toward exposition: a sophisticated ability to think conceptually, deductively and sequentially; a high valuation of reason and order; an abhorrence of contradiction; a large capacity for detachment and objectivity; and a tolerance for delayed response.[16]

But then, Postman notes, "toward the end of the nineteenth century, . . . the Age of Exposition began to pass and the early signs of its replacement could be discerned. Its replacement was to be the Age of Show Business."[17] By the "Age of Show Business" he meant a time when most communication and public discourse began to be framed in a theatrical context. Consequently, instead of appealing to the intellect, discourse began to be aimed largely at emotional stimulation; and, as John MacArthur notes, entertainment began to emerge "at the very center of family and cultural life."[18]

When the technology of television appeared in America, "it found in liberal democracy and a relatively free market economy a nurturing climate in which its full potentialities as a technology of images could be exploited."[19] In a few years television sets became a centerpiece in almost every

American home, and with little effort—merely turning on a switch— and virtually no cost to the user (except the cost of the set), Americans could assuage their growing thirst for emotional stimulation and entertainment any time they wanted.

Is Something Wrong?

Many assume that the modern worshiper's boredom with traditional services is a natural and reasonable reaction against archaic forms, style, and language. I would suggest, however, that their boredom with traditional worship is a symptom of a deeper, spiritual problem. As MacArthur states,

> If you get bored in church, may I suggest to you that it's not a commentary on the sermon—it's a commentary on your heart! Even if the sermon isn't particularly worth listening to, the chance to pick up some truths about God that come through, and then to meditate on them, should be the most exhilarating time of your life. If you're uninterested or indifferent, it's not a commentary on the sermon, it's a commentary on you.[20]

What is the spiritual problem which is symptomized by the modern worshiper's passionate quest for emotional stimulation through entertainment? Primarily, I believe it signals that a shift has taken place in his primary focus of worship—away from God and toward his own interests. Instead of viewing worship primarily as an occasion to give honor and praise to God, it signals that modern worshipers tend to view worship largely as an occasion to get something for themselves. In other words, they view worship largely as an occasion to serve themselves rather than God. Still another way of describing this spiritual problem of many modern worshipers is that they have placed themselves at the center of worship.

The modern worshiper's self-serving view of worship can often be heard in some of the simple statements he makes.

For instance, as noted earlier, one "baby boomer" explained why she returned to church after a long absence by saying, "What I decided I needed in a church was a spiritual experience at worship and communion. . . ."[21] Note that she did not return because she came to the realization that God was worthy to be worshiped. Instead, she returned primarily in order to get something for herself, namely "a spiritual experience."

Jack Lewis suggested that if modern worshipers went to public services primarily to worship God, there would be much less criticism of traditional services. Unfortunately, as Lewis observed, instead of going to worship to "call on the Lord," they tend to go and say, "Here I am, what can you do for me?"[22] Consequently, if a service does not give them the personal payoff they want, they tend to denounce it as "irrelevant," divorce themselves from it, and find one that will.

The fact that many modern worshipers have placed themselves at the center of worship is also clearly reflected in the common refrain that they will attend public worship if churches will simply design their services to give them something they want. It is obvious from the writings of those who observe the way modern worshipers think that worshiping God simply because He is worthy of worship is not a sufficient reason for many to get out of bed. George Barna, one of the nation's most noted and quoted church growth consultants, implied this mind set when he was asked to "put some of his marketing ideas into practice by helping organize a new non-denominational church." Barna said services at the church would be "at 6:00 p.m. because the 'young thinking adult' the church wants to reach won't get up for Sunday morning worship."[23]

The tendency of modern worshipers to use sacred things as a means of self-aggrandizement is so obvious that even Gary Trudeau, the writer of "Doonesbury," recently satirized it in one of his comic strips. The opening scene finds Scot, the "thirty-something" preacher for a contemporary church, sitting on the porch of the church building, drinking a cup of coffee, and thinking, "So little time. So many scheduled events!" The scene then shifts, and Scot is shown addressing the congregation. He begins, "Okay, flock, I thought I'd run through this week's activities. This Monday, of course, we have a lecture on nutrition from Kate Moss' personal chef. Tuesday and Thursday will be our regular 12-step nights." Someone in the assembly then asks, "Scot, would that be drugs or sex addiction?" Scot responds, "Drugs. Sex addiction we've cut down to nine steps. That's on Friday at 6:30 P.M.—right after organic co-gardening. Also, a special treat—Saturday night will be aerobic male bonding night! So bring your sneaks! Any questions?" A member then responds, "Yes, is there a church service?" Scot answers, "Cancelled. There was a conflict with the self-esteem workshop."[24]

Before closing this chapter, let me emphasize that the problem being discussed here is not desiring emotional uplift from worship. I am sure most of us desire, at some level, the emotional inspiration that so often comes from an encounter with God. The problem, in part, is making emotional gratification one's primary goal in worship. In other words, it is going to worship in order to receive emotional uplift as much as, if not more than, going in order to declare the magnificence of God.

The other part of the problem is seeking emotional uplift apart from the substance of worship. Remember, it's not so much through an encounter with God that many modern worshipers are seeking emotional gratification, but largely through entertainment.

Questions to Guide Study

1. Describe in your words a traditional worship service.

2. What do you think many modern worshipers are seeking from the public worship experience? Why do you think this?

3. Do you think the modern generation in general is addicted to entertainment? What has led you to this conclusion?

4. Do you think the primacy of entertainment in contemporary American culture has influenced the way many people view public worship? Explain.

5. Do you think the modern generation's boredom with traditional worship is indicative of a spiritual problem? If so, what do you think that problem is?

6. Discuss the statement, "If modern worshipers went to worship to 'call on the Lord' there would be much less criticism of traditional services." Do you agree with this statement? Why or why not?

Endnotes

[1]Andrew Hill, *Enter His Courts With Praise: Old Testament Worship For the New Testament Church* (Nashville: Star Song Publishing), ix.

[2]Ray Waddle, "Some Pews Fill; Others Grow Empty: Denominational Ties Changing, Study Says," *The Tennessean*, 16 January, 1994, 1A and 2A.

[3]Ray Waddle, "Baptist Congregation's Loss Is Another's Gain: Changes Shake-Up Nashville Churches," *The Tennessean*, 23 January 1994, 1B-2B.

[4]Ray Waddle, "Boomers Demand Own Spiritual Paths: Prodigal Sons, Daughters Want Changes If, When They Return to Fold," *The Tennessean*, 11 April 1993, 14A.

[5]Ray Waddle, "Fun and Forgiveness: Churches Urged to Adapt to New Generation," *The Tennessean*, 5 July 1991, 2A.

[6]Neil Postman, *Amusing Ourselves to Death: Public Discourse in the Age of Show Business* (New York: Penguin Books, 1985), 87.

[7]Ibid.

[8]Ibid., 80.

[9]Ibid., 86.

[10]Ibid., 116-117.

[11]Ibid., 87.

[12]Ibid., 92-93.

[13]Ibid., 148-149.

[14]NBC Nightly News, 5 November 1994.

[15]Postman, 63.

[16]Ibid.

[17]Ibid.

[18]John MacArthur, Jr., *Ashamed of the Gospel: When the Church Becomes Like the World* (Wheaton, IL: Crossway Books, 1993), 67.

[19]Postman, 86.

[20]John MacArthur, Jr., *True Worship*, John MacArthur's Bible Studies Series (Chicago: Moody Press, 1982), 89.

[21]See endnote 4.

[22]Jack P. Lewis, "Old Testament Word Studies in Worship," Speech given at the 1994 Freed-Hardeman University Lectures, audiocassette.

[23]Ray Waddle, "Pollster Warns Of Church In Crisis," *The Tennessean*, 29 December 1991, 2A.

[24]Gary Trudeau, "Doonesbury," The Tennessean, 19 June 1994, Comic Section.

Chapter 2
Walt Disney World Worship

For the past several years many churches have responded to the modern worshiper's demand for excitement and emotional gratification by adopting a new format for their public services. In these services, John MacArthur notes that traditional preaching "is being discarded or downplayed in favor of newer means, such as drama, dance, comedy, variety, sideshow histrionics, pop-psychology, and other entertainment forms."[1] Likewise, majestic melodies and anthems are being discarded in favor of modern music with driving beats, pulsating rhythms and loud dynamics. Services which are being framed in this way are often referred to as "contemporary services."

Before further discussion, it is important to understand exactly what I mean by the term "contemporary services." When I use this term, or terms such as "contemporary model" and "contemporary worship," I am referring to a worship assembly which utilizes a contemporary *style and* a contemporary *format*. What is the difference between a contemporary *style* and a contemporary *format*?

As far as *style* goes, the most defining characteristic of a contemporary service is the music. As just stated, songs in a contemporary service are often characterized by driving beats, pulsating rhythms, and loud dynamics. Slow and "soft" songs are used sparingly in most contemporary services.

Another fundamental style characteristic of a contemporary service is the general mood or tone of the service. Like the music, the overall mood in a contemporary service is generally kept "upbeat" at all times. Not only is the music designed to promote an "upbeat" mood, but the teaching is as well. Messages are almost always kept very simple and very positive, and they are typically delivered with a great deal of energy and enthusiasm. Anything that may cause sadness, anxiety, or great emotional discomfort is generally minimized.

A third fundamental style characteristic of a contemporary service is the ambiance. The notion of "formal" is completely at odds with a contemporary style. Informal dress is encouraged at all times in a contemporary service, and words like "casual" and "relaxed" are the words most frequently used by proponents of these services to describe the atmosphere they wish to achieve and maintain.

What is a contemporary *format?* Contemporary formatting can basically be described as "packaging" the activities of public worship in forms which are designed, at least in part, to entertain. Two such forms are dramatic productions (i.e., plays) and performance music (i.e., soloists, quartets, choirs, etc.). Because these forms are designed, at least in part, to entertain, it would not seem to be a misnomer to refer to a contemporary format as an entertainment format.

Some may challenge the assertion that reshaping public worship according to the contemporary model is done, at least in part, to excite or entertain worshipers. Defending this position, however, would seem difficult since many proponents of contemporary services unambiguously state that this *is* a primary aim. Consider, for example, a statement made by the "Director of Programming and Performance Arts" at one church in Arizona. In the journal *Worship Leader* he proposed that churches establish creative groups to "help research songs, dramas, and other forms of communication *to keep services exciting* (emphasis added)."[2]

Some may also challenge the assertion that a contemporary format is fundamentally an entertainment format. This too would seem an insupportable position since many leading proponents of the contemporary format basically concede that it is. For instance, consider what Bill Hybels of the Willow Creek Community Church said in a recent interview with Peter Jennings of ABC News. Jennings said to Hybels, "It didn't feel to me at all religious to be in the auditorium, it's really more like a theater. Is that intentional?" Without hesitation Hybels responded, "Yes." Then, as Jennings talked with some who attend the church, he was told by one worshiper, "It's like going to a movie, only better."[3]

Since leading proponents of the contemporary worship movement, like Bill Hybels, acknowledge that contemporary services are intended to look and feel like live theater, Quentin Schultze's description of them as "TV-styled services" cannot seriously be challenged. Schultze observes:

> As the congregation becomes an audience, the worship service is presented as entertainment. Across the Protestant and Roman Catholic spectrum, local congregational worship seems more and more like a Hollywood production . . . show-business elements are unmistakable in contemporary worship. The key words used by advocates are 'relaxed,' 'informal,' 'interesting,' and 'relevant'—but the inevitable result is TV-styled services.[4]

Perhaps Alan Walworth most colorfully captures the entertainment design of the contemporary format when he refers to it as a "Walt Disney World" model. His exact words are,

> What wisdom is gleaned for worship planners from these prototype churches and their surveys of unchurched America? Keep the mood and tempo of worship upbeat. Resist the minor keys, they're too somber. Discard 'churchy' anthems and hymns. . . . Provide sermons with catchy 'How to . . .' titles.

Encourage casual dress and informal ambiance. Drive the beat of worship with percussion, conclude songs with a flourish of high notes and loud dynamics (no one feels compelled to clap after slow or soft music). . . . We don't allow any music in our church to which you couldn't rollerskate. The new model for efficiency and friendliness and enthusiasm is Walt Disney World.[5]

Many proponents of the contemporary format may object to Walworth's assessment as an unfair caricature of contemporary worship, but the promotional material distributed by some who have adopted this format seems clearly to support his contention. For example, two brochures from one such church (the Bellevue Community Church in Nashville, Tennessee) list the following reasons why people like to attend their services: "People dress for comfort;" " We have cool music (no people in polyester singing sadly)"; "You'll have fun . . . (we didn't listen when they told us church was supposed to be boring)." One of the brochures promotes a ten-week "How to" sermon series entitled "Mastering Your Emotional Monsters," and the other a ten week "How to" sermon series entitled "The Top Ten Mistakes Married People Make . . . And How to Avoid Them."

Similarly, two brochures from another such church (the Highland Park Church in Nashville, Tennessee) list the following reasons to "try them on": "Dress for comfort (505 blue's, docker's or a three-piece suit);" "Our Pastor uses easy to understand language not 'Church-Talk'"; he also does not "preach 'at you'" or "spit, scream and yell"; "We focus on 90's problems without being boring;" "State of the art video, graphics, drama in comfortable theater seats"; and ". . . you'll love our free coffee, soft drinks and doughnuts." One of the brochures promotes a "How to" sermon series entitled "Energize Yourself" which promises to deal with such topics as how to have job satisfaction, overcome disillusionment, be happy, improve your home, manage your time, and be a friend.[6]

When Did It All Start?

When did the trend of framing public worship in an entertainment format begin? Although it may appear to be a relatively recent development, it is in fact a practice that is more than a century old—at least in American church history. Andre Resner notes that in the mid-nineteenth century, the frontier revival form of worship—which he said, "began to take on a circus atmosphere"—was beginning to be a burgeoning movement on the American continent.[7]

He points out that this form of worship was adopted when the main function of the public assembly shifted from an occasion for worshiping God to an occasion for bringing in converts (i.e., evangelizing the unchurched). In order to bring the masses into the public assembly where they would be exposed to simple messages designed to convert, a fierce pragmatism began to shape the public assemblies. This pragmatic bent said do whatever in worship "works," and "works" was "defined primarily in terms of mathematics. If the numbers are up—attendance, baptisms, and contribution—then whatever formula is used in accomplishing such mathematical ballooning is acceptable." "Successful worship," Resner notes, "became judged by the canons of numerical measurements."[8]

Once this revision in public worship began, it did not take long for it to extend from the sparsely populated frontier landscape to mainstream churches in more populous areas. James F. White describes this transition:

> In America, the Reformed tradition endured a fresh attack, this time from the new Frontier tradition. . . . Out of such occasions on the American frontier grew the practice of camp meetings, which fostered a new form of ministering ultimately systemized as revivals. Ironically, it was an erstwhile Presbyterian, Charles G. Finney (1792-1875), who brought revival patterns into the mainstream of Presbyterian church life on the more sedate East Coast. The consequence was a further erosion of the historical consciousness among

Presbyterians and a discarding of almost everything particularly characteristic of Reformed worship in favor of revivalistic patterns.[9]

Toward the end of the century more and more mainstream Protestant churches were adopting an entertainment format or entertainment elements for their public services. Like their frontier counterparts a few years earlier, they saw it as a means of attracting the unchurched masses to the Christian faith. John MacArthur notes that these churches "were not trying to hit at the core of biblical faith; they were simply trying to make Christianity more palatable to a cynical world."[10]

Some, however, including the illustrious Baptist preacher Charles Spurgeon, saw this trend as a threat to Biblical Christianity. In a series of articles which came to be known as "the Down-Grade Controversy," Spurgeon warned people of the dangers of moving away from the historic positions of biblical Christianity.[11] In his journal *The Sword and the Trowel*, he suggested that Biblical truth is like the pinnacle of a steep, slippery mountain—once a church or an individual gets on the down-grade, momentum tends to take over and recovery can only occur when Christians get on the "up-line" through spiritual revival. In 1887, concerned about the growing use of entertainment elements in public worship, Spurgeon issued a strong warning:

> The fact is, that many would like to unite church and stage, cards and prayer, dancing and sacraments. If we are powerless to stem this torrent, we can at least warn men of its existence, and entreat them to keep out of it. When the old faith is gone, and enthusiasm for the gospel is extinct, it is no wonder that people seek something else in the way of delight. Lacking bread, they feed on ashes; rejecting the way of the Lord, they run greedily in the path of folly.[12]

A few months later he would write further on the subject:

> The extent to which sheer frivolity and utterly inane
> amusement have been carried in connection with some
> places of worship would almost exceed belief. . . .
> There can be no doubt that all sorts of entertainments,
> as nearly as possible approximating to stage-plays, have
> been carried on in connection with places of worship,
> and are, at this present time, in high favour. Can these
> promote holiness, or help in communion with God?
> Can men come away from such things and plead with
> God for the salvation of sinners and the sanctification
> of believers? We loathe to touch the unhallowed sub-
> ject; it seems so far removed from the walk of faith and
> the way of heavenly fellowship. In some cases the fol-
> lies complained of are even beneath the dignity of
> manhood, and fitter for the region of the imbecile than
> for thoughtful men.[13]

Unfortunately, Spurgeon and others were "powerless to
stem this torrent," and almost seven decades after
Spurgeon's protests, A.W. Tozer addressed the situation:

> For centuries the Church has stood solidly against
> every form of worldly entertainment, recognizing it
> for what it was—a device for wasting time, a refuge
> from the disturbing voice of conscience, a scheme to
> divert attention from moral accountability. For this
> she got herself abused roundly by the sons of this
> world. But of late she has become tired of abuse and
> has given over the struggle. She appears to have
> decided that if she cannot conquer the great god
> Entertainment she may as well join forces with him
> and make what use she can of his powers. So today
> we have the astonishing spectacle of millions of dol-
> lars being poured into the unholy job of providing
> earthly entertainment for the so-called sons of heav-
> en. Religious entertainment is in many places rapid-

ly crowding out the serious things of God. Many churches these days have become little more than poor theaters where fifth-rate 'producers' peddle their shoddy wares with the full approval of evangelical leaders who can even quote a holy text in defense of their delinquency. And hardly a man dares raise his voice against it.[14]

Today, more than forty years after Tozer penned these words, framing worship in an entertainment format is more popular than ever. Reflecting on the popularity of this format, MacArthur notes:

When Charles Spurgeon warned about those who 'would like to unite church and stage, cards and prayer, dancing and sacraments,' he was belittled as an alarmist. But Spurgeon's prophecy has been fulfilled before our eyes. Modern church buildings are constructed like theaters ('playhouses,' Spurgeon called them). Instead of a pulpit, the focus is a stage. Churches are hiring full-time media specialists, programming consultants, stage directors, drama coaches, special-effects experts, and choreographers.[15]

Spurgeon would no doubt be nauseated if he could witness the lengths to which modern churches have gone to ensure that their public services are entertaining. Consider just a few examples. An article in *The Wall Street Journal* described the public service of one church as follows:

Eluding the hellfire and smoke surrounding his pulpit, the Rev. Tommy Barnett waves goodbye. With a hearty 'Hallelujah,' he soars straight toward heaven and out of sight.

The abrupt flight of this Pentecostal Peter Pan in a gray suit brings gasps from many of the 6,500 faithful at Phoenix First Assembly. Joining the extravaganza are a $500,000 special-effects system, 200-

member choir and a 25-piece orchestra. It's a finale fit for the mecca where one of Mr. Barnett's assistant pastors studies how to make such miracles happen: Bally's casino in Las Vegas. . . .

He packs the pews with such special effects as his recent flight toward heaven on hidden wires, cranking up a chain saw and toppling a tree to make a point in another sermon, the biggest Fourth of July fireworks display in town and a Christmas service with a rented elephant, kangaroo, and zebra.[16]

The same article profiled another so-called "mega-church" and its preacher. Referring to the preacher it stated, "His services are filled with showmanship: laser-light special effects that feature an actor portraying Christ's ascension, camels and donkeys at the Christmas pageant, and often a 10-piece orchestra backing up 150 choir members."[17]

Another *Wall Street Journal* article profiled still another church which acknowledged that its services were designed for a generation of churchgoers who "care passionately" about, among other things, "dazzling entertainment."[18] It described their public services as follows:

Second Baptist . . . prefers to call itself the 'Fellowship of Excitement,' on signs and in its church bulletins. . . .

Every week, Mr. Young [the preacher] and his staff critique 'game films' of Sunday's service for pacing and liveliness. An associate pastor recalls being chided once for exhorting his audience to 'raise your hands up'—the redundant 'up' slowed the service by a vital second. . . .

When it comes to worship, there is something for everyone. . . . a Sunday morning sermon series entitled, 'How to Make Your Marriage Sizzle.' . . . For a hipper, mostly single crowd, there is 'P.M. Houston,' a Sunday evening service with guitar sing-alongs and lights that transform the sanctuary from aqua to rose. Wednesday nights, older folks gather for traditional hymns and preaching at the 'Ripple Creek Gathering,' while, in a separate chapel, teenagers sway and clap at 'Solid Rock,' a service in which a rock band sings Christian lyrics.[19]

The article went on to report that in an effort "to perk up attendance at Sunday evening services," the church, "staged a wrestling match, featuring church employees. To train for the event, 10 game employees got lessons from Tugboat Taylor, a former professional wrestler, in pulling hair, kicking shins and tossing bodies around without doing real harm."[20]

Similarly, a recent article in *The Tennessean* entitled "Tightrope Walker Testifies of Christ's Role in Easter" reported that a crowd of 3,000 watched a "tightrope walker in quiet awe yesterday during Easter services held under a blue and white circus tent at First Baptist Church" in Franklin, Tennessee. The article told how this "sixth-generation Flying Wallenda" preached to the audience while performing such feats as standing on a chair on the wire. Those present "craned their necks for a better view" as he "performed." The report concluded by saying that the tightrope walker and his family "squeeze shows like this in between regular performances at fairs and circuses."[21]

One more example should suffice. The journal *Worship Leader* recently profiled a church considered to be on the cutting edge of contemporary worship. Of course, live dramatic productions are a centerpiece of their services. The author of the article, who happened to be the "Director of Programming," for the church, stated:

> The majority of our dramas came from outside sources; however, we did encourage original scripts. Spoofs on familiar characters proved to be popular. Wayne and Garth, Rich the copy man, and the church lady from 'Saturday Night Live' are all characters that baby busters are drawn to immediately. We also used themes such as 'Star Trek: The Next Generation.'

Most recently, we did a takeoff of David Letterman's 'Man in a Bear Suit' routines. To promote inviting friends to church, we dressed a man in a rented gorilla suit and placed him on the Illinois State University campus. Our question? 'Can a man in a gorilla suit invite someone to New Community?' We then video taped several segments showing the gorilla handing out cards with service information, until finally he was successful. We showed the segments at an appropriate point in the service and then introduced the invitee (with gorilla) to the congregation. For accepting the invitation, we presented the invitee with a bag of cookies, which we offer to all our first time guests. Because of the risk of embarrassment, we also presented him, before the congregation, with a can of Spam and McDonald's gift certificates. The technique proved to be relevant and to the point ('If a man in a gorilla suit can invite someone to church, why can't you?'), . . . [22]

Some may argue that such spectacles as these are extreme and not representative of most contemporary services. While that fact must be conceded, it seems clear that most contemporary services are essentially scaled-down versions of these lavish productions. For instance, instead of ten-to-twenty-five-piece orchestras, a centerpiece of most contemporary services (excluding those in our fellowship) is a band of varying size to drive the beat of the service with drums, guitars, electronic keyboards, synthesizers, and other instrumentation.[23] Also, instead of 150 to 200-voice choirs, most contemporary services utilize soloists, duets, quartets, choirs, and other types of performance music. Finally, instead of $500,000 special effects systems which can create smoke and fire, most who have adopted the contemporary model use some sort of props, staging, and special effects to create their own theatrical productions.

These facts naturally lead me to conclude that the contemporary model so popular in modern evangelicalism—as well as in some congregations within our fellowship—is the same model used by these "mega-churches" to produce their "extreme" services. It seems the only real difference between the services of these mega-churches and the services of most churches which have adopted the contemporary model is that the mega-churches have exploited the contemporary format's full potential (no doubt largely due to the financial and personnel resources uniquely available to churches their size).

Questions to Guide Study

1. How would you describe a contemporary worship model?

2. Do you think the contemporary worship model utilizes an entertainment format? Explain.

3. Explain the difference between a *style* of service and a *format* of a service.

4. Consider the services of the "mega-churches" which were profiled in this chapter. If you *don't* think such services are appropriate, do you think anything positive can be said about them? Explain.

5. If you *do* think that such services are appropriate, is there anything about them that concerns you? Explain.

6. Do you see any similarity between the public services of these "mega-churches" and those of smaller churches that have adopted the contemporary worship model? If so, what are they?

7. Why do you think churches adopt a contemporary format for their public services?

Endnotes

[1]John MacArthur, Jr., *Ashamed of the Gospel: When the Church Becomes Like the World* (Wheaton, IL: Crossway Books, 1993), xiii.

[2]Jeff Mullen, "Churches Many Services Help Meet Multiple Needs," *Worship Leader* Vol. 3 No. 6 (November/December 1994): 12.

[3]*In the Name of God*, ABC News Special Report, aired 17 March, 1995.

[4]Quentin J. Schultze, *Televangelism and American Culture* (Grand Rapids: Baker Book House, 1991), 211.

[5]Alan W. Walworth, *Journal of the American Academy of Ministry* (Fall 1992). Quoted in the "Obiter Dicta" section of the journal *Christian Studies* No. 13 (1993): 59.

[6]All of these brochures are in my possession.

[7]Andre Resner, "To Worship or To Evangelize? Ecclesiology's Phantom Fork in the Road," *Restoration Quarterly* Vol. 36 No. 2 (2nd Quarter, 1994): 67-68.

[8]Ibid., 68.

[9]James F. White, *Traditions in Transition* (Louisville, Kentucky, 1989), 72-73.

[10]MacArthur, 23.

[11]Ibid., 21-22. MacArthur's Appendix contains an overview of the "Down-Grade" articles and a fuller account of the controversy.

[12]Charles Spurgeon, "Another Word Concerning the Down-Grade," *The Sword and the Trowel* (August 1887): 398.

[13]Charles Spurgeon, "Restoration of Truth and Revival," *The Sword and the Trowel* (December 1887): 606.

[14]A.W. Tozer, *The Root of the Righteous* (Harrisburg, PA: Christian Publications, 1955), 32-33.

[15]MacArthur, 71.

[16]Robert Johnson, "Heavenly Gifts: Preaching a Gospel of Acquisitiveness, a Showy Sect Prospers," *The Wall Street Journal*, 11 December 1990, A1 and A8.

[17]Ibid.

[18]R. Gustav Niebuhr, "Mighty Fortresses: Mega-Churches Strive to Be All Things to All Parishioners," *The Wall Street Journal*, 13 May 1991, A1 and A6.

[19]Ibid.

[20]Ibid.

[21]Russell V. Gerbman, "Tightrope Walker Testifies of Christ's Role in Easter," *The Tennessean*, 17 April, 1995, 1A.

[22]Bruce Thede, "How One Church Reached Out to Baby Busters," *Worship Leader* Vol. 3, No. 4 (July/August 1994): 37.

[23]It must be noted, however, that some influential preachers in our fellowship openly argue that instrumentation is both appropriate and acceptable in Christian worship. While, as LaGard Smith says, it may only be a trickle now, "the direction we're headed is easy to see from all the background vocal imitation of musical instruments by our more contemporary singing groups" (LaGard Smith, *The Cultural Church* (Nashville, TN: 20th Century Christian, 1992), 191).

Chapter 3
Smoke Signal Services

Despite the fact that an entertainment format for public worship *may* facilitate numerical growth, *may* help a congregation maintain a numerical position, or *may* make some other seemingly positive contribution, there are several reasons why churches may want to rethink adopting such a format. This chapter, as well as the next, will explore some of these reasons.

It Reinforces the Modern Worshiper's Man-Centered, Self-Serving View of Worship

True worship is in its very essence God-centered, not man-centered. In short, this means that worship is *primarily* an occasion to serve God, not man. It means that worship must primarily be *to* God, *about* God, and *for* God.

A person's worship will be God-centered only when confessing God's infinite worth, expressing gratitude and devotion to Him, and declaring adoration for Him are the *primary* reasons for worshiping. And this will happen only when a person looks beyond his own personal tastes and interests and focuses on God—*His* Holiness, *His* power, *His* wisdom, *His* sovereignty, *His* goodness, and the wonders of *His* working in nature and history.

Unfortunately, as observed earlier, a shift has taken place in many modern worshipers' focus of worship. Instead of focusing primarily on God, many modern worshipers focus primarily on themselves. The result of this shift in focus is that their worship is corrupted—regardless of how often or sincerely they call on God. After all, as Roy Zuck observed, "Self-serving worship is no worship at all."[1]

With this in mind, one of the most fundamental objections I have to adopting an entertainment format for worship is that it reinforces this man-centered, self-serving view of worship. By asking modern worshipers what they want from worship and then carefully crafting the service to meet their demands, churches reinforce the modern generation's belief that the primary purpose of worship is to serve themselves. In this respect it is much like what happens when a parent gives a child that is throwing a tantrum exactly what that child wants. Regardless of how well-intentioned the parent's response may be, in the end it simply reinforces the child's inappropriate behavior. Similarly, regardless of how well-intentioned a church's decision to adopt an entertainment format may be, in the end it simply reinforces the modern worshiper's erroneous and unbiblical view of worship—that it is primarily a self-serving event.

Rather than giving in to the modern generation's demand to make worship more fun and emotionally stimulating, churches need charitably and patiently to call them to examine their attitudes toward worship. They need to teach them what it really means to worship God. Modern worshipers must be taught that "however much God is mentioned, worship becomes human- and self-centered, not God-centered, when its focus becomes the experience of the worshiper rather than the praise and adoration of the one worshiped."[2] Instead of feeding the modern generation's quest to "get something out of worship," churches must teach them that, as Michael Weed says,

> In its very essence, Christian worship is necessarily and inescapably God-centered, not man-centered. . . .

To forget, neglect, or diminish the God-centered nature of worship inevitably alters its basic meaning and purpose. . . . When God is no longer worshiped because he is God but because he is somehow useful, worship is no longer God-centered. Regardless of how often or sincerely 'God' is invoked, worship becomes man-centered when it is employed as a means for manipulating divine power to attain human goals (even if these are seemingly worthy goals).[3]

Only when modern worshipers learn to look beyond their own interests and focus on God will they be able to worship acceptably and grow spiritually; and only when they stop worshiping primarily in order to get a personal payoff and realize that worship is primarily an occasion to serve God will they begin to experience the full and true blessings of worship. Unfortunately, as long as churches continue to adopt entertainment elements in order to provide the emotional stimulation and excitement they demand, modern worshipers will continue to focus on themselves and believe that the primary purpose of worship is to serve themselves rather than God.

It Cannot Adequately Convey the Deep Christian Truths That Are Essential for Full Spiritual Development

A Christian's spiritual growth and development are determined in part by the amount of Christian truth that he knows and understands; and reaching full maturity as a Christian requires the knowledge and understanding of some rather complex truths. For instance, why does man need a savior? Why does God allow evil to exist and affect innocent people? How can God be in control of all things, while man, at the same time, can exercise a real choice? Who is the Holy Spirit, what is His work, and how does He work? If one is saved by grace and salvation is a free gift, why is it that not everyone will be saved? What is the relationship between Christian immersion, faith, grace, and good works in salvation? What is the nature of Scripture? What is the nature of heaven and hell? Unless a person moves beyond the elementary concepts of Christianity and begins to grapple with these deeper Christian truths, he will never reach full maturity or his full potential as a Christian. Consequently, he will always be among those who are most vulnerable to Satan's schemes.

Unfortunately, as a means of communication, entertainment simply cannot adequately convey the more complex truths of the Christian faith. In fact, only the most elementary concepts and truths can be communicated through entertainment. Given this fact, it is no wonder that many proponents of contemporary worship are in favor of doing away with deep Christian teaching in their public services. Entertainment and deep content are largely incompatible. In fact, they are so incompatible that it is virtually impossible for them to exist simultaneously; either entertainment must go, or deep content must go. Unfortunately, given this choice, more and more churches are opting to jettison deep content.

To illustrate the fact that some mediums of communication cannot convey complex concepts, consider the primitive technology of smoke signals. As Neil Postman points out:

> While I do not know exactly what content was once carried in the smoke signals of American Indians, I can safely guess that it did not include philosophical argument. Puffs of smoke are insufficiently complex to express ideas on the nature of existence, and even if they were not, a Cherokee philosopher would run short of either wood or blankets long before he reached his second axiom. You cannot use smoke to do philosophy. Its form excludes the content.[4]

Like smoke signals, entertainment is insufficiently complex to express ideas that require deep reflection and careful analysis. Consider the children's television program *Sesame Street* on this point. *Sesame Street* may be able to teach children their A-B-C's and 1-2-3's by means of an entertainment model, but it cannot utilize such a model to teach advanced mathematics, philosophy, or quantum physics. Such advanced concepts as these demand a medium that can accommodate them, and entertainment simply cannot do so: "its form excludes the content." Similarly, while an entertainment format *can* certainly communicate elementary Christian truths, it *cannot* sufficiently address the harder questions and deeper truths of Christianity. The advanced concepts of Christianity, like advanced math or philosophy, demand a medium that can accommodate them, and again, entertainment simply cannot do the job: "its form excludes the content."

If entertainment cannot accommodate the advanced concepts of Christianity, what communication media can? The fact is, there is only one medium of communication that is capable of *fully* conveying the deep truths of Christianity— *verbal* discourse. In fact, discourse as a medium of instruction can accommodate the full spectrum of Christian truth, from the most elementary truths to the most complex truths. There can be little doubt that this is partially why discourse dominated early Christian assemblies (Colossians 4:16; 1 Thessalonians 5:27; 1 Timothy 4:13; Acts 20:7); and this is also partially why discourse should continue to be a central feature of modern worship assemblies.

If Christians are going to develop spiritually to the point of reaching their full potential, they must be exposed to the whole counsel of God. Unfortunately, this cannot happen in churches that frame their services in an entertainment format. Whether these churches are conscious of the dire consequences or not, by restricting the depth of material that can be and is presented, they are directly contributing to the stunted spiritual growth of an entire generation.

It Tends to Diminish the Sense of Awe and Reverence That Should Be Present in an Encounter with God

An encounter with God is serious business, and those who choose to come into His presence must do so with reverence and awe. The Holy Spirit makes the following exhortation: "Therefore, since we receive a kingdom that cannot be shaken, let us show gratitude, by which we may offer to God an acceptable service with reverence and awe, for our God is a consuming fire" (Hebrews 12:28-29).

If God were to manifest Himself visibly or audibly in some way today, such exhortations would be unnecessary— at least for those to whom He manifested Himself. If He were to manifest Himself to someone today in a visible or audible way, awe, reverence, and even dread would be the natural and spontaneous response of that person. The Scriptures clearly bear out this effect of His presence. For instance, when God manifested Himself with thunder and lightning at Mt. Sinai, the Scripture says that "all the people who were in the camp trembled" (Exodus 19:16). When Isaiah witnessed God's majesty, he cried, "Woe is me, for I am ruined! Because I am a man of unclean lips, And I live among a people of unclean lips; For my eyes have seen the king, the Lord of hosts" (Isaiah 6:5). When Job was confronted with the majesty of God, he confessed his lack of understanding and worshiped, saying, "I retract and I repent in dust and ashes" (Job 42:1-6). When Peter witnessed a miracle which validated Jesus' identity as Messiah, he fell on his face and exclaimed, "Depart from me, for I am a sinful man, O Lord" (Luke 5:8). And when John turned around to see the voice that was speaking to him—the voice of Christ—he "fell at his feet as though dead" (Revelation 1:12-18).

God, however, has chosen not to manifest Himself in such direct ways today. Nevertheless, worship is still very much an encounter between God and His people, and as such the occasion *must* be characterized by reverence and awe. With this in mind, services that are largely designed to be fun and exciting do little to promote a sense of awe and reverence for God *or* the occasion of worship.

A casual, light-hearted service full of side-show histrionics and jazzy rhythms may promote feelings of "awe" in response to the quality and showmanship of the service, but not in response to the infinite and transcendent God. A service that more closely resembles a pep rally, a party, or the theater may generate pleasant feelings but not awe and reverence—at least not to the extent that the nature of God demands. Instead, such services can create a sense in worshipers that the occasion of worship—an encounter with God—is a rather common and ordinary event.

When worship has all the depth and look of a television show and is stripped of sacred tones and sacred words, the awe and reverence that ought to result from an encounter with God are lost. Responding to the church whose services were described earlier,[5] one researcher for the denomination expressed great concern by saying, "We can too easily lose our sense of awe, our wonder of something holy."[6] His concern is legitimate.

This is not to suggest that a person should be afraid to worship God. During His earthly ministry, Jesus clearly showed would-be worshipers that they do not need to fear Him. Some have said that the most frequent command of Jesus during His earthly ministry was "do not be afraid." While such an assertion may or may not be correct, it is certainly true that those words often fell from Jesus' lips (cf. Matthew 14:27; 17:7; 28:10; Mark 5:36). Furthermore, the Holy Spirit clearly teaches that because of the sacrifice of Christ at Calvary, people have real access to God for the first time since the fall. In other words, because of Christ's death, people can now enter with confidence the "holy place" (God's presence) to worship (Hebrews 10:19-22).

Nor is it being suggested that worship must be devoid of loud and jubilant praise. Many examples of such worship are found on the pages of Scripture. For example, Miriam and the women of Israel danced and sang praise to God in response to His deliverance of them from the Egyptians at the Red Sea (Exodus 15:20-21). The lame man whom Peter and John healed by the gate of Beautiful responded to God's work by entering the temple precincts "walking and leaping and praising God" (Acts 3:8). When one meditates upon the central truth of Christianity—that in Jesus Christ God pronounces one "in the clear" (i.e., is justified)—jubilation and enthusiasm are for him both natural and appropriate.

However, although Christians can come into the presence of God with confidence and without fear, they should not and must not enter into His presence casually or frivolously. Imagine how inappropriate it would be to meet the President of the United States with a casual and frivolous attitude. As inappropriate as that would be, it would be much more unthinkable to come into the presence of the Creator and Ruler of the universe in such a manner.

When Moses encountered God in the burning bush at Mt. Horeb (Exodus 3:1-6), he was told to stay back and take off his sandals because he was standing on holy ground. One can only imagine the sense of awe, reverence, mystery, and transcendence that must have gripped Moses as he conversed with God on that occasion. Of all the epithets that could be used to describe worship—"unique," "uncommon," and "extraordinary," perhaps this encounter yields the best way to describe it—*holy ground*. Worship is holy ground; and those who would worship God today must approach Him with no less reverence and no less awe than Moses did on Mt. Horeb. Churches that appreciate this fact will ensure that their services are presented in such a way that worshipers will know they are participating in something sacred and something demanding a disposition of awe and reverence.

When one considers the centrality of reverence and awe in true worship, of all the things that can be said against the highly liturgical public services of most Eastern Orthodox or Catholic Churches, at least one thing favorable can be said about them. They are generally framed and conducted in such a way that those who participate know that they are participating in something that demands reverence. A sense of sacredness fills their services.

Of course, this is not to suggest that we should dim the lights in our auditoriums, light candles, burn incense, erect icons, wear flowing vestments, and increase the amount of "high" ceremony in an effort to generate a sense of awe and reverence in worshipers. Although many of these elements were found in temple worship, they were conspicuously absent in first century Christian worship and should therefore remain absent in twenty-first century Christian worship as well.

The point being made is simply that a sense of sacredness and a wonder of something holy are important and essential parts of worship; and churches should consciously strive to ensure that a sense of sacredness permeates their services. How can they do this? One way is by rejecting formats and elements that would make their services resemble a Broadway production. The statement Peter Jennings made to Bill Hybels clearly shows that such services do little to promote a sense of sacredness or a wonder of something holy. As noted earlier, after visiting their services, Jennings said to him, "It didn't feel to me at all religious to be in the auditorium, it's really more like a theater. . . ."[7]

One year, after teaching a class at Wheaton College entitled "The History and Theology of Worship," Robert Webber reported that he asked his students to suggest how the material might be useful to evangelical Christians. One of their responses is worthy of serious consideration in this discussion. They replied, *restore a sense of awe and reverence, mystery and transcendence.*[8] Unfortunately, as long as entertainment is the format of choice for many churches, it will be extremely difficult to restore such an attitude—at least, as was said earlier, to the extent that God's nature and an encounter with Him demands.

Its Seems to Generally Be an Attempt to Bribe the Modern Generation to Worship

As noted earlier, it is not uncommon to hear proponents of the contemporary format argue that unless churches craft their services to give modern worshipers a desired benefit or blessing, most of them will never get out of bed or off the couch to worship. And since many modern worshipers are focused largely on having fun and feeling good when they worship, it is usually suggested that if churches hope to see the younger generation in their assemblies, they must reshape their services to make them more exciting. Hence one observes the growing popularity of adopting an entertainment format for public worship.

Those who adopt an entertainment format based on this belief—that the only way to get members of the modern generation to worship is by giving them something they want—seem clearly to be attempting to bribe the modern generation to worship. It should also be pointed out that in doing so, they appear to support Satan's assertion that man must be bribed to worship God. Roy Zuck makes this observation:

> The book of Job deals essentially with man's relationship with God, centering on two questions. The first question is, Why does man worship God? Satan suggested the motive behind Job's worship was self-focused aggrandizement (Job 1:9-11). This issue strikes at the very heart of the man-to-God relationship. *Satan's point was that God has no way of inducing man to worship him except to bribe him, to pay him in return for his devotion.* If that were true, then worship is adulterated; it is no longer man's willful adoration of God. Self-serving worship is no worship at all (emphasis added).[9]

Job's response at the end of the book, however, shows Satan's assertion to be false. When Job falls before God a broken man and worships with seemingly no expectation of having his life and possessions restored, he shows that true worshipers have always worshiped God regardless of whether or not they receive any economic, physical, emotional, or social payoff, and they always will. Job showed that true worshipers will worship God simply because He is worthy to be worshiped. In other words, Job's behavior demonstrates that true worshipers do *not* need to be bribed to worship God.

The church must keep in mind that God is seeking *true* worshipers, not just worshipers (John 4:23). Therefore, churches must resist the temptation to bribe carnal-minded people to worship by making the public worship assembly look like secular entertainment. Instead, churches need to teach would-be worshipers what it really means to worship, while at the same time ensuring that their services look like Biblical worship assemblies, not cheap—or even not-so-cheap—theater.

Its Use Generally Reflects a Lack of Confidence in the Power of the Gospel

One often hears proponents of the contemporary format argue that unless the gospel is "repackaged" to accommodate the tastes, interests, and desires of modern worshipers, the church cannot hope to move the hearts of these worshipers. Whether one realizes it or not, if a church believes that the only way the gospel will melt and move the modern generation's hearts is to put it in an entertaining "package," that church has clearly lost confidence in the power of the gospel. Instead, that church has placed its confidence in the package through which the gospel is being delivered. In other words, that church believes that the power of the gospel lies in the method and manner of its presentation as much as it lies in the message itself.

This belief is not simply *un*biblical: it is *anti*biblical. The Scriptures clearly teach that the content of the gospel alone is sufficient to move people toward Christ; it is the power of God for salvation (Romans 1:16). If the gospel is simply and clearly presented it will melt and move hearts. It is not dependent on a slick and attractive "package" for its power. This fact is clearly demonstrated throughout the New Testament (e.g., Acts 2:14-41; 8:26-40; 10:1-48; 16:11-15, 25-34).

One must reject, therefore, the suggestion that if the gospel is to be effective, it *must* be "repackaged" to accommodate the desires of modern worshipers. Contrary to popular belief, if churches will simply present the gospel in a clear, understandable, and charitable way, it will change the hearts of even modern worshipers. Of course, this is not to suggest that it will change the heart of *every* modern worshiper. The parable of the sower teaches that the gospel will be received in various ways (Matthew 13:1-23). It was received in various ways in the first century, and it will be received in various ways in the twenty-first century.

Convinced that a simple and clear presentation of the gospel can change the hearts of even the modern generation, I would suggest that churches need to stop focusing so much of their energy on how to present the gospel in fun and exciting ways in their assemblies and start focusing their energy on making sure that it is being presented in a clear, understandable, and charitable way.

Some may ask, "Didn't Paul package the gospel one way for hearers in Athens (Acts 17:22-31) and another way for hearers in Jerusalem (Acts 22:1-21)?" Yes he did. In fact, even the language he spoke while preaching to the Athenians was different from the language he spoke while preaching to the Jews in Jerusalem. Despite whatever "package" Paul's circumstances required him to use, however, all that each amounted to was a clear, understandable, and charitable presentation of the gospel. Paul was never under the illusion that more than this was needed to win people's souls. Nor must we be under such an illusion.

Questions to Guide Study

1. How could adopting an entertainment model for worship promote a man-centered, self-serving view of worship?

2. What are the limitations, if any, of an entertainment model as a vehicle of instruction and communication?

3. What kind of attitude should characterize a person who approaches God? Do you think an entertainment model promotes or prohibits such an attitude? Explain why you think this.

4. Consider the following statement: "We can't expect people to come and worship if we don't give them a good reason to come." Do you agree with such a suggestion? Do you find anything troubling about it? If so, explain what you find troubling.

5. Consider the following statement: "We must repackage the gospel if we hope to reach the modern generation." What do you understand such a statement to mean? Based on your understanding of it, do you find it troubling? If so, explain what you find troubling.

Endnotes

[1]Roy Zuck, ed. *A Biblical Theology of the Old Testament* (Chicago: Moody, 1991), 219.

[2]Michael R. Weed, "Worship and Ethics: Confession, Character, Conduct," *Christian Studies* No. 13 (1993): 500.

[3]Ibid.

[4]Neil Postman, *Amusing Ourselves to Death: Public Discourse in the Age of Show Business* (New York: Penguin Books, 1985), 6-7.

[5]See chapter 2, endnote 16.

[6]Robert Johnson, "Heavenly Gifts: Preaching a Gospel of Acquisitiveness, a Showy Sect Prospers," *The Wall Street Journal*, 11 December 1990, A1 and A8.

[7]See chapter 2, endnote 3.

[8]Robert E. Webber, *Worship Old and New* (Grand Rapids: Zondervan, 1982), 194.

[9]Zuck, 219.

Chapter 4
"'Tis Mad Idolatry"

In the last chapter I offered several reasons to rethink adopting an entertainment format for public worship. In this chapter I want to offer a few more reasons for doing so.

It Tends to Destroy a Worshiper's Appetite for Real Worship

When A.W. Tozier voiced his opposition to framing worship as entertainment,[1] John MacArthur points out his reasons for concern:

> . . . he was not condemning games, music styles, or movies *per se*. He was concerned with the philosophy underlying what was happening in the church. He was sounding an alarm about a deadly change of focus. He saw evangelicals using entertainment as a tool for church growth, and he believed that was subverting the church's priorities. *He feared that frivolous diversions and carnal amusements in the church would eventually destroy people's appetites for real worship and the preaching of God's Word* (emphasis added).[2]

The possibility that people can actually lose their appetites for real worship through long exposure to TV-styled services is very real. Those who would scoff at this danger should consider how long exposure to television shows like *Sesame Street* have affected the way many children view school. In 1969, when *Sesame Street* first aired, many parents were positively thrilled at the prospect that, by making learning fun, *Sesame Street* would teach children not only to master their A-B-C's and 1-2-3's, but also to love school.

Unfortunately, Neil Postman points out, "As a television show, and a good one, *Sesame Street* does not encourage children to love school or anything about school. It encourages them to love television."[3] The only school that *Sesame Street* teaches children to love is school that looks like *Sesame Street*. In other words, instead of stimulating the appetites of children for school, such programming actually helps destroy their appetites for it.

Today, almost thirty years later, the modern generation's appetite for school has been so thoroughly destroyed that many of them will disengage from any part of it that cannot be presented as entertainment. If they cannot physically disengage, they will do so mentally and emotionally. As a result, as noted earlier, most teachers now feel that they must incorporate entertainment into their lesson plans.

In the same manner that *Sesame Street* and similar "educational" television offerings teach children to love only school that looks like *Sesame Street*, the contemporary worship model is teaching worshipers to love only worship that looks like entertainment. In other words, it is destroying their appetites for real worship. Since it is largely through worship that one comes to see God, know God, and be inspired by God's nature and character, and since it is largely through public worship that one learns Christian doctrine, the consequences of losing one's appetite for real worship will be devastating.

When one's appetite for real worship is gone, he will consciously avoid any service that does not promise to be visually stimulating, or any service that may promote hard questions and deep reflection, or any service that may require critical analysis and complex thought. Instead, he will choose to worship only when and where he knows that the service will be fun and emotionally stimulating (i.e., entertaining). In other words, a person who loses his appetite for real worship will behave like a child who, after losing his appetite for healthy food, is given the freedom to choose what he will and will not eat. If healthy food is placed in front of such a child, he will push it away and head for the nearest cookie jar or candy dish.

When one rejects healthy food, he is depriving himself of nutrients that are essential for reaching his full genetic potential. Similarly, when a worshiper rejects real worship for a steady, uninterrupted diet of TV-styled services, that worshiper is depriving himself of spiritual nutrients that are essential for reaching his full spiritual potential. For it is a fact, as noted earlier, that entertainment is insufficiently complex to adequately convey the more complex teachings of Christianity.

Also, in addition to being deprived of many spiritual nutrients, those who opt to feast only on TV-styled services will have a difficult time "seeing" God through the smoke and mirrors of showmanship which are present in TV-styled services. And if one cannot see God clearly, one cannot know God truly; and if one does not know God truly, one can never be fully inspired, by God's nature and character, to be holy.

To sum it up and say it simply, when a person's appetite for real worship is gone, he cannot grow as a Christian. And if a person does not grow as a Christian, he cannot hope to escape Satan's snare. Satan is such a powerful adversary that spiritual growth is essential for a Christian's survival: it is not optional.

If Christians are to grow and thrive and reach their fullest spiritual potential, worship must dominate their lives. Therefore, it is imperative for churches to cultivate in their members an appetite for real worship. They can do this in part by offering services that are challenging, inspirational, and thoroughly Biblical—both in form and content. At the same time, they can do it by rejecting elements or approaches that tend to destroy people's appetites for real worship—such as the adoption of an entertainment format or entertainment elements.

With respect to this whole discussion, Cornelius Plantinga, Jr., makes an observation which is worthy of consideration. He states:

> Suppose that in your worship planning you try to keep seekers in mind, and suppose you assume that these are largely non-religious people. Suppose you further assume that if you are to appeal to these non-religious people, your contemporary services must also become increasingly non-religious, at least in any traditional way. Of course, it's hard to make a church service non-religious—it's like making a basketball game non-athletic—but for the sake of appeal to the secularists, suppose you try . . . .
>
> In general, you assume that the non-religious people like things simple and upbeat. . . . so away with lament, away with hard questions, expressions of anguish, dark ambiguities of any kind. While you're at it, away with creeds and confessions, away with explicit references to Christian doctrine, or to the history of the Christian church.
>
> On the other hand, seekers are interested in improving themselves, so you maximize promises of personal growth and self-realization. Secularists do like pop music, so here it comes into the sanctuary, along with semi-celebrity music performers and audience applause for their performances. . . .
>
> Troubling questions arise: How much of this really has anything to do with the Christian faith? . . . What if by offering popularized religion as an appetizer for unbelievers we should accidentally spoil their appetite for the real thing? Suppose your ten-year-old does not like your heart-healthy dinner menu, so you arrange a seeker meal for him in which you offer some non-threatening Pringles. You do this in order to set up his tastes buds for baked potatoes. I wonder how often that would work.[4]

It Tends to Divert the Worshiper's Attention From God to the Service Itself

Arguing for permanence and uniformity in the public worship of the church, C.S. Lewis makes the following observation:

> Every service is a structure of acts and words through which we receive a sacrament, or repent, or supplicate, or adore. And it enables us to do these things best—if you like it, it "works" best—when, through long familiarity, we don't have to think about it. As long as you notice, and have to count the steps, you are not yet dancing but only learning to dance. A good shoe is a shoe you don't notice. Good reading only becomes possible when you need not consciously think about eyes, or light, or print, or spelling. The perfect church service would be the one we were almost unaware of; our attention would have been on God.
>
> But every novelty prevents this. It fixes our attention on the service itself; and thinking about worship is a different thing from worshipping. The important question about the Grail was 'for what does it serve?' 'Tis mad idolatry that makes the service greater than the god.'
>
> A still worse thing may happen. Novelty may fix our attention not even on the service but on the celebrant. You know what I mean. Try as one may to exclude it, the question 'What on earth is he up to now?' will intrude. It lays one's devotion to waste. There is really some excuse for the man who said, 'I wish they'd remember that the charge to Peter was Feed my sheep; not Try experiments on my rats, or even Teach my performing dogs new tricks.'[5]

This same argument can be made for a stylistically simple service. A real possibility exists that a service can be so stylistically crafted that a worshiper's focus may be diverted away from God and the content of the service to the service itself. The contemporary model—by its very nature as an entertainment model—tends to do just that. An example from my own personal ministry illustrates this fact. Once, after seeing a popular "vocal band" perform, a young lady asked me if I had ever seen the group perform. When I said "no," she responded with great enthusiasm, "It was awesome; it was just like a rock concert." I then asked her what were some of the songs the group sang or what were some of their songs about. She thought for a moment and then replied, "I don't remember," and again said, "but it was awesome; it was just like a rock concert."

Musical forms such as rock, rap, jazz, and pop with their driving rhythms and loud dynamics, exciting dramatic productions with eye-catching staging and costumes, and visually stimulating videos with rapid-fire editing all have the tendency to fix a worshiper's attention on the service itself rather than God.

The potential of entertainment-styled services to divert one's attention away from God to the service itself can also be seen in the fact that when many worshipers leave contemporary services, they often have great things to say about the service but hardly utter a word about God. When worshipers leave a service with the memory of God subordinate to the memory of the aesthetic quality or exciting elements of the service, it is time to change the format. As Lewis observed, "Tis mad idolatry that makes the service greater than the god."

It Tends to Cheapen the Occasion of Worship and the Message Being Presented

Many proponents of the contemporary format maintain that if a Biblical message is presented in a service, the medium through which it is presented is irrelevant. As John MacArthur succinctly states, "That is nonsense."[6] He asks, "If an entertaining medium is the key to winning people, why not go all out? Why not have a real revival? A tattooed acrobat on a high wire could juggle chain saws and shout

Bible verses while a trick dog balanced on his head. That would draw a crowd. And the *content* of the message would still be Biblical."[7] Sadly, he notes, it is not terribly different from what many modern church leaders will do to today in an effort to entice people who are uninterested in worship to come to the public assembly.[8] The newspaper article cited earlier which reported how a tightrope walker preached while performing acrobatic stunts at the First Baptist Church in Franklin, Tennessee, would seem to vindicate MacArthur's assertion.[9]

Contrary to what many proponents of an entertainment-styled service may believe, the medium through which a message is presented does matter; it is very important. If for no other reason, it is important because communication media tend to assign in a listener's mind a value to the occasion in which a medium is employed, and/or a value to the message which is being conveyed by the medium.

Considering the impact of the chosen medium, it is naive to think that changing from a non-entertainment medium to an entertainment medium will have no effect on a worshiper's perceived value of worship or the message that is being presented. When worship is presented as entertainment, it will inevitably reduce, in a person's mind, the significance of this encounter with God. That is, those who are regularly exposed to entertainment styled services are almost certain to develop a more casual view of worship than those who are not. In other words, they will likely come to view worship not as the highest, most exalted, and most profound activity that man can engage in, but as a rather ordinary event. To say it yet another way, they will come to view worship and Christianity as something that should be taken seriously—but not too seriously.

It is also possible that those who are regularly exposed to entertainment-styled services will develop a more casual attitude toward the message that is being presented. Messages which are proclaimed in the Christian assembly should be messages from God. Paul told the Thessalonians, ". . . we also constantly thank God that when you received from us the word of God's message, you accepted it not as the word of men, but for what it really is, the word of God, . . ." (1 Thessalonians 2:13). Peter told his readers, "Whoever speaks, let him speak, as it were, the utterances of God; . . ." (1 Peter 4:11). If the messages of God are constantly conveyed through mediums of entertainment, it seems very likely that people will eventually fail to give them the attention and serious consideration that a message from God deserves. Another way of saying all of this is that an entertainment format will eventually destroy the dignity of worship and maybe even the dignity of the gospel.

Not long ago a popular preacher said he would be willing to dress up as Bozo the Clown if that was what it took to ensure that people would listen to the gospel. While such a comment may sound noble, it is in fact something to be concerned about. To illustrate why, consider a scenario where the President of the United States had to inform the country that it was at war. No president has ever come to such an occasion and made such an announcement in a clown suit. Why? Obviously, it would be grossly inappropriate. Such an occasion is far too serious for such a medium. If such a medium were used, it would proclaim as loudly as any words that the occasion was not worthy of serious consideration.

Coming into the presence of God with praise and adoration is the highest, most serious, and most profound activity a human being can engage in. One would surely devalue it by dressing it in the garb of cheap theater. Likewise, the message of Jesus Christ calls for more serious consideration and deeper reflection than any message ever heard, for it calls one to sacrifice his life in response to God's saving work (Romans 12:1-2). That message delivered in a clown suit, or clothed in many other entertainment forms, would make a declaration stronger than any words that it is not a very serious message. Nor would it tend to prompt the deep reflection that the message of Christ crucified demands.

In all fairness, many proponents of the contemporary format would probably agree that the use of some entertainment forms in worship can lead to inappropriate excesses which cheapen the occasion of worship and the message being presented. They would argue, however, that it is possible, and even necessary, to keep the services interesting for modern worshipers by using entertainment forms that are reverent and dignified, and therefore do not reduce the value of the occasion of worship or the gospel. In other words, in their promotion of the contemporary model they are careful to warn of the potential danger of excesses and emphasize the need for moderation.

While it is true that some forms of entertainment may be able to preserve the dignity of the occasion and communicate a simple biblical truth without cheapening it, even simple, reverent, and "dignified" forms of entertainment tend to promote a shift of focus away from God. Furthermore, they are incapable of teaching deeper Christian truths, and they tend to destroy a worshiper's appetite for worship that is not framed as entertainment. Furthermore, when a decision is made to adopt moderate, or dignified, entertainment forms for the public assembly, it would seem very difficult to maintain that moderation over a long period. Being well aware that one should be very cautious in using "floodgate" arguments,[10] and at the risk of being labeled an alarmist, I must warn that when the door is cracked enough to admit entertainment of even the most dignified sorts into the public assembly, it probably will not be long until the full potential of the medium is exploited. As Spurgeon warned, when one gets on the "down-grade," momentum tends to take over.

It Is Using Worship as a Means to an End

As noted earlier, Schultze observed, "For the sake of maintaining or building congregations, local pastors and churches have imitated the styles of entertainment popular with the generation nurtured on TV."[11] In other words, a primary reason that many churches adopt an entertainment format is to facilitate numerical growth or prevent numerical decline. What this boils down to is that many churches are using their public services as a tool to fill pews.

Worship, however, is an end in itself. The primary purpose of worship is to glorify God. Worship must never be reduced to a means by which something else is accomplished—either by individuals or by church leaders. To use worship primarily as a means of achieving attendance goals—or reaching any other humanly chosen goal, for that matter—is to corrupt the meaning and purpose of worship. A terrible tragedy occurs when congregations begin "using" their public services largely for purposes other than to glorify God and build people up in the faith.

It Has No New Testament or Historical Precedent

Entertainment occupied a high place in the first century Greco-Roman world. Its position was probably not as high as the one it occupies in twenty-first century American culture, but it was very important. The remains of massive theaters throughout Palestine and the rest of the Roman world attest to its prominence.[12] Also, Jesus' frequent use of the term "hypocrite" (Matthew 6:5; 23:13-29)—a word which originally stemmed from the world of theater and meant "a play actor"—suggests firsthand familiarity with the theater.

Given this fact, it seems rather striking, at least to me, that the early church did not utilize an entertainment format when they assembled—at least there is no real evidence that they did either in Scripture or in the uninspired writings of early "church fathers." Is this fact significant? It seems reasonable to think that if framing worship as entertainment was an appropriate option, the apostles and the early church would have exploited such a "culturally relevant" format. The fact that they did not exploit this format, however, would seem to suggest strongly that they did not feel it was appropriate for Christian worship assemblies.

Is All Change in Worship Wrong?

This challenge to the contemporary format may appear to reflect a conviction that change in the sphere of public worship is, for one reason or another, impossible; and therefore any proposed change must be rejected as inappropriate.

Such an appearance, however, could not be further from reality. Change in the sphere of public worship is not only possible, but occasionally may be necessary. Every aspect of the Christian faith, including public worship, must constantly be scrutinized under the microscope of divine revelation and adjusted, if need be, to bring it more into harmony with Scriptural truth.

It is also proper for churches to consider adopting changes to public worship that may help them better express the great truths of the Christian faith, increase a worshiper's participation in worship, make worship more "vertical" in its orientation rather than "horizontal," better facilitate the spiritual development of the worshipers, or help cultivate in worshipers an appetite for real worship. But, for the reasons delineated in the last two chapters, churches should reject the adoption of an entertainment format for their public services.

What About Just a Contemporary Style?

Earlier I suggested that, as far as worship is concerned, there is a difference between a contemporary style and a contemporary format. I now want to suggest that it is possible for a contemporary style to exist apart from a contemporary format. Given this possibility, and having just proposed several reasons to rethink adopting a contemporary format, a logical question that could be raised is, "What about adopting only a contemporary style?" I believe it all depends on whether or not the contemporary style that one wishes to adopt is what I call a "full-blown" contemporary style or a "moderated" contemporary style.

What is the difference? For one thing, the atmosphere of a moderated contemporary style service may be somewhat casual and relaxed, but it is not so casual that people forget they are worshiping God and instead think they are at a movie, a circus, a concert, or a sporting event. Also, the general mood and tempo of a moderated contemporary style service may be "upbeat," but there are still plenty of times when the mood may become solemn and the tempo may slow down; and there are plenty of times when the teaching will go beyond the elementary concepts of Christianity and deal with deeper questions and concepts. Finally, in a moderated contemporary style service the use of "contemporary music" may be a prominent feature, but "traditional" hymns with their majestic melodies and anthems, as well as slow and "soft" songs, are still regularly heard.

If this is the type of contemporary style that a church wishes to adopt, I cannot intellectually, Biblically, or emotionally object. On the other hand, if a church wants to adopt a "full-blown" contemporary style, then I have many of the same concerns that I would have if a church wanted to adopt an entertainment format for their public services.

For instance, I do not think there will be enough deep Christian teaching in a "full-blown" contemporary style service to promote a person's full spiritual development. I also think that a "full-blown" contemporary style service is so casual and informal that it tends to diminish the sense of awe and reverence that should be present in an encounter with God. Still another concern I have is that a "full-blown" contemporary style service will destroy people's appetites for any service that promotes deep reflection and hard questions. I am also concerned that a "full-blown" contemporary style service will prompt worshipers to view worship and Christianity as something to take seriously, but not too seriously.

One other concern I have is that I do not think a "full-blown" contemporary style will exist for very long apart from a contemporary format. In other words, I am confident that when a church adopts and becomes committed to maintaining a "full-blown" contemporary style, the adoption of entertainment elements (i.e., a contemporary format) will quickly follow.

Questions to Guide Study

1. Do you think it's possible that long exposure to entertainment styled worship can destroy a person's appetite for any service that is not framed as entertainment? Explain.

2. What are some dangers of losing one's appetite for non-entertainment styled services?

3. Do you think a particular communication medium has any impact on how seriously a person views a message? Explain.

4. How would you respond to someone who suggests that "dignified" entertainment forms should be utilized in worship in order to engage the interest and hold the attention of the modern generation?

5. What is the problem with adopting an entertainment format primarily in order to facilitate numerical growth or prevent numerical decline?

6. Discuss the difference between a "full-blown" contemporary style and a "moderated" contemporary style.

Endnotes

[1]See chapter 2, endnote 14.

[2]John MacArthur, Jr., *Ashamed of the Gospel: When the Church Becomes Like the World* (Wheaton, IL: Crossway Books, 1993), 68-69.

[3]Neil Postman, *Amusing Ourselves to Death: Public Discourse in the Age of Show Business* (New York: Penguin Books, 1985), 144.

[4]Cornelius Plantinga, Jr., Perspectives (May 1993), as quoted in the "Obiter Dicta" section of *Christian Studies* No. 13 (1993): 59.

[5]C.S. Lewis, "Liturgy," *The Joyful Christian* (New York: Macmillan Publishing Co., 1977), 80-81.

[6]MacArthur, 69.

[7]Ibid.

[8]Ibid., 69-70.

[9]See chapter 2, endnote 21.

[10]A "floodgate" argument, as LaGard Smith says, is an argument which seizes upon improbable ultimate consequences as a reason for not doing something that is imminently reasonable. He notes the danger in using such arguments and then uses it to argue against the uses of women in "neutral" areas such as passing a communion tray (LaGard Smith, *Men of Strength for Women of God* (Eugene, Oregon: Harvest House, 1989), 294.).

[11]Quentin J. Schultze, *Televangelism and American Culture* (Grand Rapids: Baker Book House, 1991), 211-212.

[12]The Greeks are generally credited with the beginning of the theater in the sixth and fifth centuries B.C. See the discussion on "Theater" in *Nelson's Illustrated Bible Dictionary*, Herbert Lockyer, Sr., Gen Ed. (Nashville, TN: Thomas Nelson Publishers, 1986), 1043.

Chapter 5
Defending the Delinquency

Although the primary purpose of this section was to analyze and evaluate the contemporary worship format, it would also seem helpful, before leaving the section, to evaluate some of the reasons that prompt churches to adopt an entertainment format for their public services.

How will such an evaluation be helpful? For one thing, it will help a person determine the most productive and appropriate way to discuss the subject with those who have adopted, or may be thinking of adopting, this format. As we shall see, people may adopt an entertainment format for very diverse reasons; and therefore, each individual may need to be approached a bit differently concerning the matter.

For instance, rather than being chastised, those who have adopted this format for noble reasons deserve to be commended for having worthy and honorable motives. Then, of course, they must be taught charitably and patiently why Christian worship should not be framed as entertainment. On the other hand, those who have adopted an entertainment format for less than noble reasons must be taught not only about why worship should not be framed as entertainment, but also why their reasons for adopting the format are not legitimate.

Another good reason to examine *why* people adopt an entertainment format is that serious analysis will create within people an awareness that there are some reasons for reshaping worship that simply are *not* legitimate. This clarified understanding will help people make good decisions when confronted with the dilemma of whether or not to support proposed changes in worship. It will also remind people to check their motives before proposing a change to worship. Asking the simple question, "Why do I want to do this?" can help a person know whether or not he is proposing changes in worship for legitimate reasons.

Now that this basis for study has been established, let us examine some of the reasons that more and more churches are adopting an entertainment format for their public services.

Part of a Larger Evangelistic Strategy

Some churches seem to adopt an entertainment format as part of a larger evangelistic strategy to win the modern worshiper's soul. To understand exactly what part entertainment plays in their evangelistic strategy, one must first understand the larger strategy.

The strategy works like this: first of all, a congregation does something in an effort to attract outsiders to its public services. Next, it implements measures to ensure that visitors have a positive experience and leave with a positive impression of the church; the motivating assumption is that a positive experience may stimulate an interest in spiritual matters. Finally, Bible studies are offered to those whose interest in spiritual matters are stimulated. Through these studies it is hoped that many will be converted. Reduced to its simplest terms, this strategy can be summed up as follows: get people to the services; stimulate their interest in spiritual matters, teach them the gospel.

It is in the first two phases of this evangelistic strategy that many churches utilize entertainment. Framing worship as entertainment is the "something" that many congregations do to attract visitors to their services. At that same time, it is also the primary measure they adopt to make a positive impression on their visitors. In fact, many churches seem to believe that framing their services as entertainment is about the only thing that will attract and make a positive impression on the modern generation.

Is this a valid evangelistic strategy? There is certainly nothing wrong with the basic mechanics of the strategy. Yet it must be remembered that worship is not primarily for outsiders. Therefore, its value must never be assessed from the perspective of outsiders—despite Paul's concern that worship be decent and in order in case an outsider is present (1 Corinthians 14:22-25). However, there is nothing inherently wrong with churches adopting appropriate measures, in part, to attract outsiders to their public services (e.g., showing a marriage or family enrichment film series).

Likewise, it is perfectly legitimate for a church to adopt appropriate measures to ensure that visitors have a positive experience and leave with a positive impression of the church. It is imperative to note, however, that the key word in both these statements is *appropriate*. Some measures that many use to attract and make a positive impression on outsiders must be rejected as inappropriate. Churches must never think for a moment that they are constrained only by their imaginations when it comes to attracting and making a positive impression on outsiders.

Some measures for attracting and impressing outsiders must be rejected because they violate clear Biblical teaching or principles. For instance, the message of salvation is that salvation is only in Christ and that God places a person in Christ only when one believes in Christ as Messiah, repents of his sins, and is immersed in the name of the Father, Son, and Holy Spirit. If outsiders find any part of this message so offensive that they refuse ever to visit a church that preaches it, so be it. That is the message of salvation which the Holy Spirit revealed, and no church can change that message for any reason.

Similarly, in God's plan for the functioning of His church, He has clearly assigned certain tasks exclusively to men. If outsiders find it offensive that women are not permitted, among other things, to preach to the assembly or teach a Bible class which is composed of men and women (1 Timothy 3:12-14), or that women are not permitted to lead the assembly in prayer (1 Timothy 2:8), or that they are not permitted to be elders (1 Timothy 3:1-7), or that they are not permitted to be deacons (1 Timothy 3:8-13),[1] so be it. The church cannot change this plan for *any* reason, including to attract and impress the modern generation.

There are other measures that must be rejected as inappropriate or wrong although they may not be specifically condemned in Scripture. For reasons discussed earlier, framing worship as entertainment is one such measure.

What about the notion that an entertaining service is perhaps the only way—or at least the best way—to attract and make a positive impression on contemporary outsiders? This idea could not be further from the truth. While a TV-styled service will certainly attract some outsiders to worship who would otherwise be uninterested, there is at least one drastically different measure that is not only *appropriate* for a church to use in trying to attract outsiders, but it is also *guaranteed* to attract from among the contemporary generation more visitors than any TV-styled service could ever attract.

What is this "sure-fire" way to attract outsiders to a public service of the church? It is members of a congregation extending warm, heartfelt invitations to their friends and relatives to come and worship with them. This answer may seem anti-climactic, but studies consistently show that most visitors to almost any church are there in response to an invitation of a friend or relative. Studies also consistently show that most people become members of a particular church as a result of the influence of a friend or relative.[2] Instead of trying to attract outsiders with a plethora of gimmicks— including entertainment styled services, perhaps more church leaders need to spend time encouraging, exhorting, and inspiring Christians to invite their friends and relatives to worship and Bible study.

There is more good news. Entertainment is not only unnecessary to attract outsiders: it is also unnecessary to impress them. Whether or not a visitor leaves a service with a positive impression is determined largely by how he was treated, not by how entertaining the service was. Therefore, if a church wants to make a positive impression on its visitors, it should work hard at being friendly, caring, and helpful to them.

To summarize, there is nothing inherently wrong with the evangelistic strategy that says: get people to the services, stimulate their interest in spiritual matters, and try to teach them the gospel. If churches want to use this as *one* strategy to evangelize their communities, well and good. They must never think for a moment, however, that *anything* that may draw and impress a crowd is an appropriate measure for the church to adopt.

Attract the Unchurched to Christianity

For others, the general purpose of adopting an entertainment format for worship is to attract the general public to the Christian faith. In other words, instead of being part of a larger evangelistic strategy, it *is* the evangelistic strategy. To say it still another way, making the public services entertaining seems to be the primary means that some churches use to persuade modern worshipers to follow Christ. In this respect, it appears to be much like what Constantine—the first "Christian" emperor—tried to do with church buildings more than sixteen centuries ago.

Two years after Constantine became master of the East in A.D. 324, his mother Helena made a pilgrimage to Jerusalem. Her visit initiated the construction of hundreds of church buildings in the Holy Land. Yoram Tsafrir notes that the general purpose of this massive building effort was "to impress and attract the general public to the Christian faith."[3] He states:

> When Constantine became the patron of the Christian faith and elevated it to an official, honored

status, the heads of the Church were obliged to adopt trappings befitting the imperial religion. The emperor encouraged the bishops to decorate their religious edifices to the same extent as the pagans had embellished theirs. *It was a significant step in the struggle for the soul of the masses, who hesitated between the new religion and the traditional cults.*

Although the early Christians had been comfortable with the modest *domus ecclesia* and its atmosphere of intimate fraternity and humility, values in the time of Constantine changed: *There was a desire to absorb the masses into the Christian community and to impress them by royal splendor no less than by spirituality.* The interior of the church was decorated lavishly with carved columns and capitals, mosaics and wall paintings, expensive building materials, and gold chandeliers. The priests wore elaborate liturgical vestments. The shadowy interior of the building, with burning candles and incense, gave the finishing touches to an atmosphere of mystery that is characteristic of Christian worship (emphasis added).[4]

While all would agree that winning the unchurched world to Christianity is a noble goal, one must ask, "Is trying to win them by splendor a valid evangelistic strategy?" Despite the fact that, as already asserted, framing worship as entertainment will no doubt entice some people to worship who would otherwise be uninterested, trying to win the hearts of pagans by making Christianity attractive to them must be rejected as a valid evangelistic strategy. Why? To be blunt and to the point, it is because Jesus never directed, or even suggested, that His disciples try to win the world by making Christianity attractive to the world. As some have put it, Jesus told His disciples to preach the gospel, not sell it. His instruction to the twelve was basically, "If you can't win people with substance, move on" (Matthew 10:14), not "If you can't win people with substance, try to win them with splendor."

Hoping to find some validity in trying to win people with splendor, some may note that crowds were attracted to Jesus through the splendid miracles He performed. While Jesus' miracles certainly attracted crowds, they were never done simply to dazzle people and win their allegiance. Surely this is why He refused to leap off the pinnacle of the temple into the Kidron Valley when Satan challenged Him to do so (Matthew 4:5-6). Jesus performed miracles largely to confirm His identity as Messiah and to teach spiritual truths (e.g., "I am the bread of life" [John 6:1-59], "the light of the world" [John 9:1-41], "the resurrection and the life" [John 11:1-44]), not to make either Himself or discipleship attractive.

When it came to making disciples, Jesus never tried to "sell" Himself to the world by portraying discipleship as an exciting experience or as something that would enhance people's earthly existence. Instead, He violated every rule of "marketing" theory by portraying discipleship as a life of self-denial (Matthew 10:39), potential hardship, and possible persecution (Matthew 10:17-23). In other words, He never buried the news that discipleship came with a high price in an attractive, exciting "package." He explained very carefully what it meant to be a disciple and encouraged people to count the cost before making a commitment (Luke 14:28).

On one such occasion, after Jesus told a crowd of several thousand just how high the cost of discipleship was, John reports that many walked away (John 6:53-60). Jesus' response to their decision to turn away is quite interesting, especially in light of how far many churches seem to go these days to make Christianity attractive to contemporary pagans. Rather than pursuing them with promises of convenience, ease, fun, and an enhanced earthly life if they would return, Jesus simply turned to His disciples and said, "You do not want to go away also, do you?" (v. 67).

Certainly Jesus could have gained and retained more followers had He concentrated on making the concept of discipleship a bit more attractive. But Jesus was looking for disciples; and what He would have gotten had it been His first priority to make discipleship attractive could have hardly been called such. Similarly, preachers and church leaders who make it their first priority to attract and retain people with the sensibilities of most modern worshipers may succeed in doing nothing but, as Jeffrey Peterson notes, "presiding over a weekly convention of religious dilettantes."[5] Peterson goes on to observe that unless the modern generation's attitude toward the Christian faith is challenged, "the proceeding can scarcely be called a church."[6]

Recalling A.W. Tozer's words that some proponents of entertaining worshipers can "quote a holy text in defense of their delinquency,"[7] many claim to find Biblical support for framing worship as entertainment in Paul's statement, "I have become all things to all men, that I may by all means save some" (1 Corinthians 9:19-22). A consideration of this passage in its context, however, shows that it cannot support such claims.

In this passage, Paul is encouraging the Corinthians to be willing to sacrifice their own personal liberty in order to avoid being needlessly offensive to their neighbors and brethren. Why does he do this? Because he recognizes that needlessly offending people can create an obstacle to evangelizing one's neighbors and/or promoting holiness among one's brethren. This text says nothing about what Christians should do when they gather to worship. Nor does the principle found in this text apply to what the church should do when it gathers to worship.

Consider the context. In 1 Corinthians 8:13 Paul begins his appeal by saying that he would sacrifice his own personal liberty in order to avoid being needlessly offensive to anyone. He then uses a personal example to illustrate what he is saying. In 9:1-14 he tells his readers that he has a right to receive financial support from his converts. But then, in 9:15-18, he tells them he has refused to exercise this right.

Why did Paul refuse to exercise his right to be compensated? No doubt because he feared that being compensated might impede the spread of the gospel. How could accepting compensation impede the spread of the gospel? Since

many charlatan preachers roamed the ancient world motivated by financial gain (2 Peter 2:3; 1 Timothy 6:5), Paul
probably knew that if he required compensation from his
converts, or even accepted it on some occasions, his action
might arouse suspicion in some people's minds concerning
his motives for preaching. Such suspicion would likely prevent many from giving his message serious consideration.
Therefore, to ensure that this would never happen, Paul sur-
rendered his right to be compensated. This personal example leads up to his general missionary policy of vv. 19-23. As
John MacArthur says regarding these verses,

> Paul was not suggesting that the gospel can be made
> more powerful by adapting it to a certain cultural con-
> text. He was not speaking about accommodating the
> *message*. He was simply saying he would not jeopar-
> dize his ability to preach the message by unnecessar-
> ily offending people. If the message was an offense,
> so be it: 'We preach Christ crucified, to Jews a stum-
> bling block, and to Gentiles foolishness' (1 Cor. 1:23).
> But Paul would not make *himself* a stumbling block to
> unbelievers: 'Give no offense either to Jews or to
> Greeks or to the church of God' (10:32).[8]

The lesson to the Corinthians, as Peterson says, "is that in
their difficult social situation, caught between sociable
pagan neighbors on the one hand and fellow Christians cautious of sacrificial meat on the other, they must be ready to
forsake their accustomed dining practices to avoid leading
other Christians into sin."[9] The church today must maintain
this same missionary policy. Peterson goes on to note,

> Paul's example is mentioned in connection with the
> church's *worship* not in 1 Corinthians 9:19-22 but in
> 10:32-11:2. The passage forms a transition between
> two main sections of the letter: chaps. 5-10, which
> treat various issues concerning the relations between
> Christians and non-Christians in Corinthian society,

and chaps. 11-14, which deal with problems in the Corinthians' worship assemblies. Paul's admonition in 1 Corinthians 10:32 to 'give no offense to Jews or Greeks or to the church of God' summarizes his resolution of the dispute over food sacrificed to pagan gods in chaps. 8-10. 'Giving no offense to the church of God' means in the first instance refraining from actions that will lead a fellow member of the church to violate a moral scruple.

But the admonition to 'give no offense to the church of God' also points forward, preparing the reader for what follows in chap. 11; as he introduces the topic of adornment in worship, Paul commends the Corinthians for their fidelity to the traditions that he had passed on to them (11:2), which accord with the practices of churches everywhere (11:16; cf. 4:17). One way for the Corinthians to avoid offending against the church of God is to conserve the apostolic traditions, both in worship (11:23-25) and in doctrine (15:1-11).

Throughout 1 Corinthians Paul stresses the obligations of the local church to the church universal (cf. 1:2; 4:17; 7:17; 14:33; 16:1-4). It is striking that when he turns to the service of worship he insists that his converts respect the twenty years of Christian tradition that preceded the foundation of the church at Corinth. The attitude of the apostle to the Gentiles toward liturgical tradition contrasts markedly to that of contemporary advocates of the seeker service.[10]

Instead of trying to win the world by splendor, churches must simply preach the gospel to the world—just as the apostles did twenty centuries ago (Mark 16:15-16). And as they do so, they must tell the world that, although salvation is free, it is certainly not cheap (Matthew 10:38-39). They must inform the world that discipleship demands the complete surrender of a person's mind and body to Christ (1 Corinthians 6:19-20; Galatians 2:20). They must also explain that although Christian living will no doubt enhance many aspects of a person's life, it may also bring a great deal of hardship and persecution (1 Peter 5:12-13; 2 Thessalonians 1:5-6). And they certainly must *not* forget to tell to the world that the ultimate consequence of rejecting the message of salvation is eternal destruction (2 Thessalonians 1:7-8). Finally, churches must exhort those who are considering discipleship to count the cost before making a commitment (Luke 14:25-35). Only by doing these things will churches make *real* disciples.

On the other hand, if style and splendor become the primary means through which churches attempt to win the world, pews may swell, but it is unlikely that many of these "converts" could really be called "disciples." Instead, to borrow Peterson's term, "religious dilettantes" would probably be the best way to describe them. This may satisfy some preachers and church leaders, but it will not satisfy Christ; He wants disciples (Matthew 28:19-20).

Before moving on, perhaps it would be beneficial to consider briefly why more churches than ever seem to be adopting a "win-the-world-by-splendor" strategy. The primary reason behind the adoption of this strategy by many people seems to be that they are convinced that the attention, interest, and allegiance of modern worshipers can only be won with style and splendor. In other words, churches are adopting this strategy because they genuinely believe that there is no other way to win the hearts of the modern generation.

Is this a valid belief? Not exactly, although it is easy to understand why some might think so. Raised on MTV, rock and roll, and fast-moving, visually-oriented media excellence, many modern worshipers have little tolerance or appetite for critical thinking, careful analysis, and a logical, rational approach to anything. As a result, most of them tend to measure the value of everything, including worship, by how fun or entertaining it is. Consequently, many modern worshipers simply will have nothing to do with services that do not promise to be entertaining. Given these circumstances and this mindset, there can be little doubt that framing worship as entertainment will entice many people to worship who would otherwise be uninterested.

These facts, however, do not mean that every member of the modern generation can be won only with style and splendor. There are many modern worshipers who still desire eternal life more than a fun-inducing and emotionally stimulating experience. And there are still many modern worshipers who prefer substance to style. As a result, if churches will simply present the gospel in a clear, understandable, and charitable way, the hearts of even modern worshipers will be won: There will never be as many won as one would like, but it *will* happen. Twenty centuries after it was first presented, the gospel still has the power to move the hearts of those who are disposed to eternal life (Acts 13:48).

Let me try to sum up everthing I've been trying to say in this section. Individual Christians and church leaders must keep in mind that the appeal of Christ and Christianity has always been that *it is true*. The primary appeal of following the one true God has never been that it will bring a financial windfall, or that it will always be fun, or that it will enhance one's earthly existence in some way. These things may or may not come to those who give their allegiance to Christ, but these things are not the appeal. The appeal has always simply been that *it is true*. This is indicated by Peter's response to Jesus in John 6:68. As noted earlier, when the masses turned away from Christ and left, Jesus turned to the twelve and said, "You do not want to go away also, do you?" Peter replied, "Lord, to whom shall we go? You have the words of eternal life."

When churches try to win people to Christ largely by making Christian worship a fun and exciting experience, they are changing the fundamental appeal of Christianity. They are changing the fundamental appeal of being devoted to God. They must stop. If people are not interested in following Christ because what He offers is true, we must not try to get them to follow Christ for some other reason. If people are not interested in substance, we must not try to win them with style. If people are not following Christ because He is "the way, and the truth, and the life" and "no one comes to the Father" except through Him (John 14:6), then their discipleship is a sham. If people are worshiping God largely because "it's like going to a movie, only better,"[11] then their worship is a sham.

Maintain or Increase Church Attendance

Rather than adopting an entertainment model primarily with a view toward winning the modern worshiper's soul, there is convincing evidence that many churches do so for the "less-than-noble" reasons of facilitating an increase or preventing a decline in "church" attendance. As noted earlier, Schultze contends, *"for the sake of maintaining or building congregations*, local pastors and churches have imitated the styles of entertainment popular with the generation nurtured on TV (emphasis added)."[12]

One of the *Wall Street Journal* articles which was referred to earlier contains a good example of someone adopting an entertainment format primarily for the purpose of building a numerically large congregation. In the article, one preacher explained why his congregation uses an entertainment format by simply saying, "I want the biggest church I can think of."[13] Another newspaper article which was cited earlier contains a good example of someone adopting an entertainment format primarily for the purpose of preventing numerical decline. It reported that one preacher at a large middle Tennessee workshop urged churches of Christ to adapt their services to a new generation in order to prevent their exodus. The article quoted him as saying, *"Many have left* looking for the experiential aspect of religion . . . People want to experience their faith, not just think it. Baby Boomers' lives are so filled with worry about economics and relationships, they want a place where they can flat out have some fun" (emphasis added).[14]

Even the more secular minded recognize that many of the recent changes in the sphere of "Christian" worship have been instituted in an effort to build or maintain audiences.

For instance, at the outset of the previously cited ABC News special on contemporary Christianity, Peter Jennings observed, "All across America, Christianity [is being] transformed *in an effort to keep church going alive* (emphasis added)." He then asked what has to change in traditional Christianity so that churches can "stay in business." One church leader responded by saying that "church" cannot be "all doom and gloom and all of you take your Bible now and let's just bore each other. Let's show them we can also have fun."[15]

I have even observed in my own ministry that many who consider adopting a contemporary format, or some of its basic elements, generally do so on the basis that "we must do something about our worship if we want to attract young people or young couples to our church," or "we must do something about our worship if we want to keep our young people or young couples from leaving us." Arguments such as, "it is a culturally relevant means of teaching the modern generation," or "it will attract more people to the services and thus expose more people to the gospel," often seem to be *ex post facto* arguments designed largely to buttress a decision which was made primarily on the assumption that adopting the format would improve the potential for increasing or maintaining the number of "patrons."

Why have more and more churches become so preoccupied with building and maintaining audiences? There can be little doubt that the modern church growth movement is largely responsible. For almost a quarter of a century it has convinced many church leaders to adopt public service attendance figures as the chief criterion for gauging success and to accept as *good* whatever pulls in the most people. Since framing worship as entertainment tends to pull in a crowd, the smart move is to adopt an entertainment format.

Are these valid, Biblical principles for the church to embrace? Certainly not. Attendance figures are not now, nor have they ever been, a reliable measure of a congregation's success—at least not in God's eyes. As He has always done, God measures success by faithful conformity to His will. As MacArthur notes, real success "is not prosperity, power, prominence, popularity, or any of the other worldly notions of success. Real success is doing the will of God regardless of the consequences."[16] Perhaps nowhere does Jesus more clearly state this fact than in His "Sermon on the Mount." To the multitudes which had gathered He said, "Not everyone who says to Me, 'Lord, Lord,' will enter the kingdom of heaven; but he who does the will of My Father who is in heaven" (Matthew 7:21).

David Wells observes correctly that perhaps the greatest deceit that the modern world has "successfully palmed off" on the modern church is the belief that a congregation's health lies in its flow charts, its convenience, and its offerings instead of its inner life, its spiritual authenticity, the toughness of its moral intentions, and its understanding of what it means to have God's word in this world. He also correctly observes that "the world's business and God's business are two different things."[17]

This is not to suggest that wanting to see a consistent increase in attendance at worship and Bible study is somehow inappropriate. There is nothing wrong with a church wanting to see its pews filled. It is simply saying that church attendance is *not* a factor when it comes to how God views a church. God may view with disfavor a church whose attendance is 15,000, while at the same time He may view with favor one whose attendance is barely fifteen. As stated before, it is faithful conformity to His will that God is interested in, not merely how many warm bodies are filling pews on any given Sunday.

Not only is the modern church growth movement wrong in its promotion of attendance figures as the chief criterion for gauging a church's success, but it is also wrong in its tendency to promote as *good* anything that draws a crowd. Although pragmatism may have a legitimate place in the process of determining whether or not to adopt a proposed change in public worship, that place is certainly not number one on the "checklist."

When evaluating a proposed change in public worship, the first question to ask is not, "will it draw a crowd?" but rather, "is it in harmony with Biblical truth?" (i.e., does it violate clear Biblical teaching or a Biblical principle)? If it is *not* in harmony with Biblical truth, there is no need to ask anything else. The proposed change must be rejected. If, on the other hand, it seems to be in harmony with Biblical truth, I would suggest that there are still other important questions to ask before considering pragmatic matters like "will it draw a crowd?"

Although it would be difficult to identify all these questions, one that should definitely be asked is, "Would adopting this practice create a high potential for disrupting the harmony of this congregation?" Other questions may include the following: "Would adopting this practice promote an erroneous view of worship?"; "Would it diminish the sense of awe and reverence that should be present in worship?"; "Would it help create or destroy worshipers' appetites for real worship?"; "Would it in any way cheapen the occasion of worship or the message being presented?" and "Would it divert the attention of worshipers away from God to the service itself?"

To summarize, it is perfectly legitimate for churches to want to see their pews filled. Churches must remember, however, that attendance is *not* a factor when it comes to God's viewing a congregation with approval or disapproval. Churches must also remember that the acid test for determining whether or not a proposed change to worship—or to any other aspect of the Christian faith—is "good" begins with the question "is it in harmony with the word of God?" not "will it draw a crowd?" So, while it is acceptable for churches to want to see their pews filled, they must never want to see them filled so badly that they are willing to permit worship—or any other aspect of the Christian faith—to be corrupted.

One final thought seems to be in order before concluding this chapter. Although it is legitimate for a church to want to see its pews consistently filled, churches should not pursue merely "filling pews" as one of their primary goals. Why? For one thing, God never called His people to pursue the goal of merely filling pews. Nowhere among the literally hundreds of commands of the New Testament does God ever commission His church to pursue mere numerical growth as either a primary or a secondary goal. This alone seems clearly to suggest that God is not interested merely in the number of bodies filling "church" pews each week. And if God is not interested in merely filling pews, should merely filling pews be a primary goal of the church?

Of course, some may claim Biblical support for the pursuit of mere numerical growth by noting that Luke often published conversion figures in the book of Acts. Luke, however, was not encouraging the pursuit of merely "filling pews" when he documented how many people were being converted during those early days of Christianity. Instead, he was simply letting the reader know to what extent the kingdom of God was growing in those early years despite strong opposition. Also, another important point to note is that Luke was recording actual converts and not mere pew fillers. There is a significant difference between the two.

A second reason to reject the pursuit of mere numerical growth as a primary goal is that it tends to distract people's attention and energy from the pursuit of faithfulness. Churches that make it their main mission to fill pews tend to spend a great deal of time, attention, and energy learning how to get people into their buildings and keep them there. Consequently, they have less time, attention, and energy to devote to learning God's will and applying it to their lives. As a result, not only does their understanding of God's word tend to remain rather shallow, but in these churches a careful interpretation along with the application of Scripture tends to become subordinate to pragmatism. It is not uncommon, therefore, to see many aspects of the Christian faith—like worship—corrupted in these churches.

Of course, some would no doubt argue that "filling pews" and "faithfulness to God" are both worthy goals and that churches can and should aggressively pursue both simultaneously. They would probably argue that the key is balance.

To those who may be disposed to this idea, Vernard Eller makes a comment that is worthy of serious consideration:

> Success is determined by the statistics regarding such things as membership, attendance, giving, budget, staff, facilities, and activities. Success equals the number of participants multiplied by the degree of their satisfaction and support. . . . 'Fidelity,' on the other hand, is faithfulness to the gospel, conformity to the mind of Christ, being what the biblical revelation calls the church to be. . . . The two are not so nearly alike or so intimately connected that *one* choice can include *both*. No, if the congregation chooses success *over* fidelity, then that choice is itself an infidelity, an act of unfaithfulness. If, on the other hand, the congregation chooses fidelity *over* success, success may follow *or it may not*—there is no guarantee, no promise, no assurance, and no connection. Success can and does come to churches that are completely unfaithful, and success can be created through factors that have nothing to do with fidelity.[18]

In conclusion, Peter Kreeft also makes an observation that is very relevant to this entire discussion. He says, "Jesus commanded us not to succeed, but to obey; not to sell the gospel, but to proclaim it. . . . It is not our job to convert the world or to fill churches; that is God's job. Ours is to sow the seed, without sugar-coating it; God's is to make it take root and grow.[19]

Questions to Guide Study

1. Identify some reasons that more and more churches are adopting an entertainment format for their public services.

2. What is the first question that should be asked when a change to worship is proposed? If a proposed change does not seem to violate Biblical teaching or a Biblical principle, what are some other questions that should be asked before adopting the proposed change?

3. What would you suggest are some appropriate measures that a church may use to attract outsiders and make a positive impression on them?

4. Read 1 Corinthians 9:19-22. Does this passage lend support to framing worship as entertainment? If not, what does it mean for the church today?

5. Do you believe it's possible for a local church to have many *worshipers* on any given Sunday yet have few *disciples*? Explain the difference.

6. Do you believe the attention, interest, and allegiance of the modern generation can only be won with style and splendor? If so, to what extent do you think individual Christians and churches should respond to this?

7. Should the church aggressively pursue numerical growth as one of its primary goals? Why or why not?

Endnotes

[1]Some argue, based largely on 1 Timothy 3:11, that there were women deacons in an official sense in the New Testament church. Although the probability is slim that *gunaikas* in this verse should be understood as "women deacons," the possibility cannot be dogmatically rejected. However, even if the word does refer to women serving in an official sense, the principles of the New Testament (1 Timothy 2:12) would clearly prohibit them from functioning in any sort of position of leadership or authority over men.

[2]After surveying 14,000 "church members," the Institute of American Church Growth reported that 75-90% of them became members of their particular church as a result of the influence of a friend or relative (*Leadership and Church Growth International* seminar notes, Rapid City, SD, 21 September 96).

[3]Yoram Tsafrir, "Ancient Churches in the Holy Land," *Biblical Archaeology Review* Vol. 19 No. 5 (September/October 1993): 30.

[4]Ibid., 31-32.

[5]Jeffrey Peterson, "How Shall the Seeker Say Amen?" *Christian Studies* No. 13 (1993): 22.

[6]Ibid.

[7]See chapter 2, endnote 14.

[8]John MacArthur, Jr., *Ashamed of the Gospel: When the Church Becomes Like the World* (Wheaton, IL: Crossway Books, 1993), 96-97.

[9]Peterson, 26.

[10]Ibid., 26-27.

[11]See chapter 2, endnote 3.

[12]See chapter 2, endnote 4.

[13]Robert Johnson, "Heavenly Gifts: Preaching a Gospel of Acquisitiveness, a Showy Sect Prospers," *The Wall Street Journal*, 11 December 1990, A8.

[14]See chapter 1, endnote 5.

[15]*In the Name of God*, ABC News Special Report, aired 17 March, 1995.

[16] MacArthur, 29.

[17]David F. Wells. *God in the Wasteland*. Grand Rapids: Eerdmans, 1994.

[18]Vernard Eller, *The Outward Bound*. Quoted in the "Obiter Dicta" section of the journal *Christian Studies* No. 13 (1993): 57.

[19]Peter Kreeft, *Back to Virtue*. Quoted in the "Obiter Dicta" section of the journal *Christian Studies* No. 13 (1993): 57.

Section Two
Contemporary Trends

Chapter 6
Drama

In his book *Ashamed of the Gospel*, John MacArthur observes that throughout the evangelical community preaching "is being discarded or downplayed in favor of newer means, such as *drama,* comedy, variety, side-show histrionics, pop-psychology, *and other entertainment forms*" (emphasis added).[1] He also observes, as was noted earlier, that "modern church buildings are constructed like theaters. . . . Instead of a pulpit, the focus is a stage. Churches are hiring full-time media specialists, programming consultants, stage directors, drama coaches, special-effects experts, and choreographers."[2]

Although most churches of Christ currently do not utilize drama in their public services to the extent that many churches in the larger evangelical community do, drama in public worship definitely has its proponents and practitioners in churches of Christ. For instance, one well-known writer contends that some churches trying to stay in touch with their culture may find drama to be the best means of communication for their particular setting.[3]

Another strong proponent of drama in public worship basically argues that modern Americans have been raised in such a way that they have largely lost the capacity—or at least the will—to think logically, abstractly, sequentially, or continuously over extended periods of time. As a result, he contends that traditional sermons tend to fall on deaf ears. He argues that it is "time for us to come out of the Dark Ages with regard to communicating with people in our churches and larger communities."[4] He further argues that "in today's visual culture, a six-minute piece of drama . . . can have more 'punch' in awakening people to their spiritual needs than a forty-minute sermon."[5] Finally, he states that in this "nonliterary culture that thinks in sound bites rather than sequentially," the church must learn to use forms of communication such as drama "for the sake of the gospel message it [this culture] needs to know."[6]

Despite the fact that a dramatic production may draw bigger crowds, or that it may help keep the attention and interest of some modern worshipers, or that it may make some other seemingly positive contribution, I am convinced that dramatic productions should be reserved for occasions other than the public worship assembly. Why? Some would suggest that the practice should be rejected in worship because it lacks New Testament precedent. In other words, they reject it because they find no authority for it in the New Testament. Those who hold this view should be commended for wanting to ensure that everything done in worship has Biblical authority.

Proponents of drama, however, may argue that although drama is not specifically authorized in Scripture, it is authorized under the general command to "teach." In other words, they may argue that Jesus told His disciples to teach but left it to their discretion to choose what medium might best accomplish that task in any given circumstance. In all fairness, this argument seems to have some legitimacy.

If drama can be considered a legitimate means of instruction, why then should we reject it in public worship? One must not assume that *every* legitimate means of instruction is necessarily appropriate for Christian worship. There may be several reasons that disqualify a particular vehicle of instruction from being used in public worship; and for reasons discussed in the last section, I am convinced that drama falls into this category.

This is not to suggest that dramatic productions have no place in the life of the church. On the contrary, I am convinced that they do. One place that drama is certainly appropriate is in forums for instructing children. Children's Bible classes and Vacation Bible School would be two such forums. As a teacher of pre-school children, I have frequently dressed my students in period costumes to reenact great Biblical stories.

Dramatic skits may also be considered appropriate on occasions other than during the corporate worship assembly—perhaps as a "special program." In this respect it would be much like the common practice of a college chorus or a special singing group performing for a congregation following their evening or morning worship assembly.

Some may think that rejecting drama in public worship but promoting its use elsewhere in the life of the church is inconsistent, but it really is not for several reasons. For one thing, children's Bible classes are not worship assemblies. The thesis of the last section was that it is inappropriate to frame Christian *worship* as entertainment. It was never suggested that it is inherently wrong to communicate Bible stories and Bible truths through entertaining media.

Also, although worship must *never* be used as an occasion to entertain people, there is absolutely nothing wrong with church leaders providing their congregation and the larger community with Christian entertainment on occasions other than public worship. In fact, I would suggest that churches with adequate resources may want to consider periodically providing their members with some sort of "Christian" entertainment; even adults need an occasional entertaining diversion from the difficult and exhausting challenges of life. And given the fact that much of the entertainment being offered today promotes worldliness and immorality, entertainment that contains a Christian message, promotes holy living, or stimulates a person to read and study his Bible is desperately needed.

There is at least one more reason why I do not feel that it is inconsistent to reject drama in worship but promote its use elsewhere in the life of a church, and that is, there is a significant difference between the mental development of a child and that of an adult. The mental development of a child essentially requires more of an entertaining approach to education. In other words, the mental development of a child requires lessons that are simple, visually interesting, and very short. Adults, on the other hand, have the capacity not only to think abstractly, but also to focus their attention for longer periods of time. Unlike children, adults are mentally equipped to handle media of instruction that can more thoroughly teach Christian truth.

Perhaps on this point it might be helpful to consider the suggestion that modern Americans have been raised in such a way that they have been rendered largely unable, or at least unwilling, to think abstractly, logically, sequentially, and continuously for long periods of time. Is this true? First, no one could seriously challenge the idea that modern American culture is a nonliterary culture—especially when compared to other cultures and other periods of American history. Second, no one could seriously challenge the notion that modern Americans generally think in visual images rather ti..an abstractions.

Despite these facts, however, *most* modern Americans have not totally lost the capacity, or the will, to think logically, abstractly, sequentially, or continuously for long periods of time. Most Americans do not require ideas to be communicated through dramatic productions in order to understand and appreciate them. This conviction stems primarily from the observation that the bulk of ideas in the political, business, military, and educational arenas are still communicated through verbal discourse. And although much of this discourse is supported by some form of visual imagery (e.g., color slides and videos), the fact still stands that drama has not replaced discourse as the primary means of communication even in this overly-stimulated, visually-oriented culture. This fact alone seems clearly to suggest that modern adult Americans have both the capacity and the will to think logically, abstractly, and sequentially. The fact that you, the reader, are doing all of these things at this very moment proves the point.

On this point, let me offer a suggestion for your consideration. If members of the modern generation really are less skilled than those of previous generations when it comes to thinking logically, abstractly, sequentially, and for extended periods of time, why cave in to such mediocrity? Why should churches of Christ not lead the way in teaching their young people to do these things and do them well?

Can anyone really deny that children who are taught to sit quietly in periods of worship are already more capable of sitting for extended periods outside worship? And can anyone really deny that children who grow up singing four-part harmony are generally better at it than children who do not have that early experience? What we need to be more creative about is not how we entertain our young people in worship, but how we teach them to think in ways their MTV friends do not.

What about the often cited support for drama which asserts that people are more likely to remember and comprehend what is being taught if a presentation is supported by some sort of visual image(s). To the extent that this is true, drama is not the only means of providing visual images that will help listeners remember and comprehend what is being taught. There are at least two other ways to provide reinforcing and supporting visual images without having to frame worship as entertainment—stories and visual aids. Incidentally, both of these have Biblical precedent. In fact, Christ Himself set these precedents.

First, consider stories. Christ frequently told stories (Matthew 13; 25:1-30). The Bible calls most of them parables. A well-told story can create in the mind's eye as vivid and clear a picture as any dramatic presentation could ever create. Good preachers, therefore, will frequently tell good stories to illustrate the Biblical truths they are trying to convey.

Second, consider visual aids. Jesus often used them. For instance, when the Herodians and Pharisees tried to trick Him with a question about taxes, Jesus asked to see the coin used to pay the poll-tax. When they gave Him a denarius, He held it up and asked, "Whose likeness and inscription is this?" (Matthew 22:15-22). On another occasion when the disciples asked Him, "Who then is the greatest in the kingdom of heaven?" the text says, "He called a child to Himself and set him before them, and said, 'Truly I say to you, unless you are converted and become like children, you shall not enter the kingdom of heaven. . . .'" (Matthew 18:1-5).

As far as visual aids are concerned, more preachers should make frequent use of them in the pulpit. As already suggested, this would increase the likelihood that listeners would remember more and comprehend better what was being taught. For instance, if someone wanted to preach on the parable of the ten virgins (Matthew 25:1-13) he might want to bring a replica of a first-century Roman oil lamp and a flask such as would have been used to carry extra oil. If someone wanted to preach on Matthew 24, he might want to show color slides of what Jerusalem and the temple would have looked like during Jesus' life, or slides of archeological evidence of the Roman destruction of Jerusalem in A.D. 70. The possibilities for good visual aids are almost endless, and they have the potential to significantly impact listeners in a positive way. If they did not have a strong potential for making a positive impact on listeners, Christ certainly would not have used them.

Some, thinking that drama and visual aids are essentially the same thing, may be wondering how a person can so strongly support the use of visual aids in public worship, yet reject the use of drama. Although drama and visual aids may have some things in common—they both present visual images to an audience—there are clear differences between the two.

For one thing, the purpose of visual aids is always to support preaching, never to supplant it. Visual aids rarely stand alone because they generally cannot stand alone; and they generally cannot stand alone because they are generally not intended to stand alone. Instead, they are usually intended to function in a support role. Drama, on the other hand, is generally intended to be a stand alone form of communication, and as such it is often adopted, as MacArthur suggests, as a replacement for what is largely felt to be an irrelevant form of communication in the modern age—preaching.[7]

A second difference between drama and visual aids is that drama is clearly a form of entertainment. That is, dramatic skits are designed largely to entertain people. The fact that they may also be designed to teach a moral lesson does not diminish the fact that they are designed also to entertain. Visual aids, on the other hand, are not typically designed to entertain people. This does not mean that they cannot be used to entertain people, it simply means that they are not typically designed to do so. Consider, for instance, the occasions referred to earlier where Jesus used visual aids. When he held up a coin by way of illustration (Matthew 22:15-22), He was obviously not trying to entertain the masses. Instead, He was laying a foundation to make an important point. And when He used a child to make His point (Matthew 18:1-5), He was obviously not trying to entertain them. Instead, He was using the child to help them understand an important truth.

Before concluding this section on drama, I feel constrained to revisit a suggestion made by one leading proponent of drama in the public services of churches of Christ. He stated, "In today's visual culture, a six-minute piece of drama . . . can have more 'punch' in awakening people to their spiritual needs than a forty-minute sermon."[8] Although this suggestion may sound valid, it seems to reflect a belief that causes me some concern. It seems to reflect the belief that the power of the gospel lies primarily in the package in which it is delivered.

As discussed earlier, however, such a belief is simply not true. While the gospel must be clearly and thoroughly presented before it can work, its power does not lie in the delivery system. The power in the gospel is the gospel itself

(Romans 1:16). That is, the message that Christ died, was buried, and then was resurrected is itself the power that changes and shapes lives. With this in mind, I am convinced that a clear, careful, and thorough presentation of the gospel delivered through verbal discourse (i.e., a sermon) will have as much "punch" in awakening modern worshipers to their spiritual needs as a presentation of the gospel in drama will—at least it will in modern worshipers who are truly disposed to eternal life.

Questions to Guide Study

1. Is it valid to assume that any legitimate means of instruction is appropriate to use in a public worship setting? Support your answer.

2. Do you think dramatic productions have a legitimate place in the life of the church? If yes, give examples of when you think it would be appropriate to utilize them.

3. What are two ways that teaching in public worship can be supported by visual images without adopting an entertainment format? Give Biblical examples of each.

4. What are some fundamental differences between visual aids and dramatic productions?

Endnotes

[1]John MacArthur, Jr., *Ashamed of the Gospel: When the Church Becomes Like the World* (Wheaton, IL: Crossway Books, 1993), xiii.

[2]Ibid., 71.

[3]Lynn Anderson, *Navigating the Winds of Change* (West Monroe, LA: Howard Publishing Co., 1994), 84. In all fairness to brother Anderson, in this book he does not seem to aggressively promote the adoption of drama in the public assembly. Instead, he simply presents it as a legitimate and viable option for teaching in the assembly.

[4]Rubel Shelly, "A Responsible Challenge to Our Traditions," chap. in *In Search of Wonder: A Call to Worship Renewal* (West Monroe, LA: Howard Publishing, 1995), 86.

[5]Ibid.

[6]Ibid., 87-88.

[7]Ibid.

[8]See endnote 5.

Chapter 7
Contemporary Music

There has been a great deal of spirited discussion among brethren in recent years over the use of contemporary music in the public worship assembly. One writer has vigorously promoted the adoption of such music largely on the basis that "many church-goers find 'church music' boring and unrelated to life. And for the unchurched visitor, our music is a foreign language."[1]

The same writer asks, "What should we do when young people are leaving us in droves because we are not connecting with their heart language and when hundreds of searchers check out our churches but don't come back because they don't understand the 'foreign language'?" He contends, "If the church connects with this . . . world, it must speak a variety of 'musical heart languages.'"[2] He says that "in order to communicate in the changing heart languages of the people, musical styles must . . . keep changing,"[3] and, "to connect with today's heart language, we will need more contemporary music."[4] He explains contemporary music as "that which is common right now, current," and lists "country, rock, pop, etc." as examples.

Others have resisted the adoption of contemporary music in the assembly for a variety of reasons. Some may resist it because they believe such music is theologically anemic.

Others may do so because they believe many of the rhythms of contemporary music are largely inappropriate for the divine assembly. Still others may resist it because they do not believe that accommodating the demands of modern worshipers is a precedent they wish to set. A few may even reject it simply because they are uncomfortable with anything new or different in the assembly.

As LaGard Smith suggested, however, much of the resistance to contemporary music seems largely to be based on a concern that contemporary music means "contemporary doctrine."[5] In other words, it is not contemporary music *per se* that most object to. It is simply that many see such a close relationship between contemporary music and contemporary doctrine that they believe the adoption of the former may lead to the introduction of the latter; and not wanting to see contemporary doctrine come through the doors, they are reluctant to let contemporary music through the doors.[6]

Although such a concern may be legitimate, I believe many contemporary praise songs possess at least two characteristics that make their use in worship highly desirable. At the same time, however, I am convinced that the *exclusive* use of such music in the worship assembly is highly undesirable. In the remainder of this section I will attempt to explain these propositions as well as propose a criterion for selecting appropriate songs for worship.

One characteristic that makes some contemporary songs desirable is their strong vertical orientation. This fact is reflected in their frequent identification as "praise songs." Since worship is primarily an occasion to ascribe adoration and praise to God, songs of adoration and praise should be a prominent part of the church's lyrical response in worship.

This is not to suggest that praise and adoration should be the only forms of lyrical response heard in the public assembly. On the contrary, it is important to ensure that expressions of praise are *not* the only verbal expressions heard in the assembly. Among other things, when Christians assemble, they should recite in their songs the story of redemption, they should recount in them the works of God in creation and human history, they should proclaim in them their expectation of Christ's return, and in them they should provoke one another to righteous living. It is simply being suggested that, since worship is an occasion to ascribe honor and praise to God, verbalizing praise—while not the only feature of public worship—should be a central feature of it.

Nor am I suggesting that there are no traditional Christian hymns which are vertically oriented. Some of the most priceless hymns of praise are those which have been sung for decades or even centuries. A terrible tragedy would occur if these songs ceased to be sung when the church assembled simply because their composition pre-dates the birth of most modern worshipers. What I am suggesting is that there are many contemporary songs which could be incorporated into the church's existing repertoire to enhance and broaden the selection of praise songs from which to choose.

A second characteristic which makes the use of some contemporary songs desirable is their simple melodies. Some hymns have such complex musical arrangements that great concentration and effort are required to sing them properly. Speaking from personal experience, this can not only draw a worshiper's focus away from God or the message of the song, but also leave one exasperated and frustrated.

Most would probably agree, however, that many contemporary songs have melodies which can be picked up rather quickly and easily retained. By freeing worshipers of the need to grapple mentally with difficult musical arrangements, such melodies would seem to allow worshipers to bring their fullest concentration to bear on the content of the songs they are singing.

Despite these desirable characteristics, however, it would be a tragic mistake for the church completely to jettison its traditional hymnody in favor of contemporary praise songs. This conviction is based largely on the fact that, as some have noted, many contemporary songs simply "do not tell the story very well." That is, they tend to be more theologically hollow than traditional Christian hymns. Put still another way, they do not contain the volume of Christian doctrine that many traditional hymns possess.

Instead, as the term "praise songs" suggests, they often consist largely of repeated expressions of praise and adoration. As a result of their limited theological content, an uninterrupted diet of such songs may contribute to a spiritually malnourished generation and a hollow church. Of course, this is not to say that *all* contemporary songs are theologically hollow. It is simply saying that contemporary praise songs in *general* contain much less theology than many of the hymns which were composed by earlier generations of believers.

Unlike many contemporary songs, most traditional hymns are so theologically rich that in past generations the hymnal often served the church as a fount of instruction in Christian doctrine. For centuries Christians, through their songs, recited the story of redemption, recounted the works of God in creation and human history, proclaimed the certainty of Christ's return, described in majestic fashion the attributes of God, provoked one another to focus on things above, encouraged one another to live holy lives, beseeched God's mercy, petitioned His help and guidance, acknowledged unworthiness, mourned their sinfulness, repented of their sins, confessed Christ as Lord, and sounded the praises of Father, Son, and Holy Spirit. Through such a wide and varied lyrical response, if someone failed to learn Christian doctrine by reading his Bible, there was still hope that he would learn it through the songs which were sung when the church assembled.

Today, not only are people *not* reading their Bibles, but when they do go to worship, they are often fed an uninterrupted diet of theologically "lite" praise songs. As a result, the present generation is quickly on its way to becoming the most Biblically illiterate generation in American history. In view of this frightening trend, there seems to be a greater need than ever for singing songs that are rich in Christian doctrine when the church assembles.

Both contemporary praise songs and theologically rich traditional hymns have great things to offer the church when it gathers to worship. I believe most churches would enrich their worship by utilizing appropriate songs from both categories. Of course, this raises the question, "What constitutes an appropriate song?" Common sense and Biblical principles suggest that an appropriate song from either category has several characteristics.

One, an appropriate song will reflect a basic theme or insight into Christian theology or the Christian experience. On this point consider the song "America the Beautiful." I have been in worship assemblies where this song was sung. Although it is certainly a beautiful song, one cannot help but to ask, "Exactly what theme or insight into Christian theology or experience does this song reflect?" Since the answer has to be "none," such songs are not really appropriate for Christian worship.

Two, the text of an appropriate song will be in harmony with Scripture. Unfortunately some songs reflect a less than exact understanding of Biblical truth. Worship leaders must always "be on the lookout" for these instances and take the appropriate action when they are identified. What is the appropriate action? That depends on the circumstances. If it is simply a short phrase within a song that is unbiblical, the leader may make a brief comment about it before leading it. If an entire stanza of a song is not in harmony with Scripture, and yet the other stanzas are Biblically sound, the leader may want to make an annotation in his book and refrain from leading that stanza. After all, there really is no need to jettison an entire song simply because of one questionable stanza. Finally, some songs may be so thoroughly filled with unbiblical teaching that they cannot be "rehabilitated." In such a circumstance, worship leaders have no other choice but to remove the song from the church's repertoire.

Three, an appropriate song will not reflect an excessive emphasis on selfish concerns. An excessive emphasis on self is incompatible with the Christian faith. Christians are to lose themselves for Christ's sake (Matthew 10:39), deny themselves (Matthew 16:24), and be willing to give up all they have for Christ (Luke 14:33). In other words, a Christian places his entire life under the control of Christ. The songs that Christians sing when they assemble ought to reflect this attitude.

Four, the rhythm of an appropriate song will express the tone or the feelings of the lyrics. For instance, the rhythm of song that proclaims and celebrates one's privileged status as a child of God should not sound like a funeral dirge. Similarly, the rhythm of a song that confesses one's weakness and petitions God for strength and mercy should not sound like a victory celebration.

Five, the language of an appropriate song will be clear and understandable. It is imperative that people understand what they are singing. If people do not understand what they are singing, how can they truly be edified? On this point, perhaps something needs to be said in reference to some of the older hymns that are frequently sung in most congregations. There are words and phrases in many of those songs that most of us modern worshipers simply do not understand. The following excerpt from a bulletin article written a few years ago brings this point home in a very humorous way:

> . . . alas the area of our singing has become a trysting place for me. I've spent many a direful night, rent assunder, with ebon pinion brooding o'er the vale. What e'er betide, the bowers will not fail, even from ether-plains. It's time to raise our Ebenezers and fain become gladsome. In mirth we have moaned, our suits disdained. Now is the time to have our spiritual thirst assuaged as we fain the supernal among the zephyrs wafting in the dale from days of yore.[7]

I am not suggesting that hymns containing such phrases be rejected as inappropriate for public worship. Even as they correct unbiblical doctrine in a song, leaders simply need to explain the meaning of uncertain words and phrases in a song prior to leading it. Of course, if a leader does not know the meaning of an uncertain phrase in a particular song, he *should* stop leading that song—or at least the stanzas which contain those words and phrases—until he educates himself.

Six, an appropriate song must have a musical arrangement—a rhythm—that is appropriate for entrance into the divine assembly. I am convinced that some rhythms simply are not appropriate for an encounter with God because they lack the dignity and reverence that an encounter with God demands. In this connection, perhaps a word needs to be said in response to one writer's suggestion which was cited earlier. He said that, when it comes to music in worship, the church needs to adopt more "country, rock, pop, etc."

It is difficult to assess precisely what he is proposing since many different rhythms can be heard within each of these categories of music. In each category there are songs that can be found with rhythms that are hauntingly beautiful, majestic, dignified, and reverent. At the same time, however, there are songs that can be found in each category with rhythms that are light years away from reverent and dignified; one may encounter a beat that, to borrow Allan Bloom's words, "makes the body throb with orgasmic rhythms."[8]

If the suggestion means that the church needs to utilize the entire spectrum of rhythms found in these categories of music, then his suggestion must be rejected. After all, most would probably agree that country rhythms like "Boot Scootin' Boogie," rock rhythms like "Born to Be Wild," and pop rhythms like "Beat It" are hardly appropriate for entrance into the divine assembly.

Before concluding this discussion on appropriate rhythms or melodies in worship, let me raise a question that some may have never considered, and that may warrant some thoughtful reflection. Do the songs a person chooses to sing as he worships say anything about his view of God? I am convinced that it does. I believe that if a person chooses to sing songs to God which are generally characterized by reverent, majestic melodies and anthems, it reflects a reverent, majestic view of God. On the other hand, I cannot help but believe that if one's music of worship is largely sung to beats which, again to borrow Bloom's words, "makes the body throb with orgasmic rhythms," it reflects a less than majestic view of God. Perhaps we need to think deeply on this matter as we select the songs through which we will approach and worship God.

In conclusion, as suggested earlier, both contemporary and traditional songs have something worthy to offer the church as it attempts to worship God. As also suggested, many churches may find that their services would be enriched by utilizing *appropriate* songs from both traditional and contemporary categories. The key word in this matter, as in virtually every matter, is *balance*.

Questions to Guide Study

1. What would you consider to be some strengths and weaknesses of "contemporary music?"

2. What would you consider to be some strengths and weaknesses of "traditional music?"

3. Do you think praise should be the only lyrical response to the church's singing? If yes, why do you think this? If no, why do you think this, and what other verbal expressions should be made through the songs a church sings?

4. In your opinion, what constitutes an appropriate song for Christian worship?

Endnotes

[1]Lynn Anderson, "Music That Makes Sense," *Wineskins* Vol. 1, No. 9 (Jan/Feb 1993): 27.

[2]Ibid.

[3]Ibid.

[4]Ibid.

[5]LaGard Smith, "How We Worship," lecture given at the 1995 David Lipscomb University Lectures, audiocassette.

[6]By the term "contemporary doctrine" I mean such things as questioning the saving significance of Christian immersion, identifying as "Christian" and extending virtually full fellowship to many who have never been immersed, suggesting that instrumental praise is an acceptable and appropriate expression of Christian worship, and promoting a wider role for women in public services to include such things as singing solos, leading prayers, and even preaching.

[7]Church bulletin of the Broadway Church of Christ, Lubbock, TX (29 July 1990).

[8]Allan Bloom, *The Closing of the American Mind* (New York: Simon & Schuster, 1987), 73-75.

Chapter 8
Lifting Hands

One of the latest trends in worship on the evangelical landscape is lifting hands in a manner that traditionally has been a feature of charismatic services. This was recently implied during the previously cited ABC News special on contemporary American Christianity. The host, Peter Jennings, said:

> *What you will see here* [he was referring to an influential church in California], *is part of the fastest growing trend in contemporary Christianity*. It is called experiential or charismatic Christianity. The idea is to come and have an emotional, often *physical*, encounter with God. . . . *The Vineyard* [the name of the church to which he was referring] *says stand up and reach out* (emphasis added).[1]

While Jennings made this observation, a camera panned an audience in which most of those present were standing with their arms raised and hands extended.

In addition to its growing appeal in the larger evangelical community, lifting hands in worship is also finding a favorable audience in churches of Christ. For instance, one writer suggested that people raise their hands during private prayer in order to experience something that would enrich their worship. His exact words were, "In the privacy of your home, worship the Lord using your hands. . . . Raise your hands as you pray . . . See if your communication with him is not enriched."[2]

In the same article the writer recounted a strong church-shaping lesson taught by one man who, after the congregation had sat down following a period of high-spirited praise songs, "remained standing on the second row with his eyes closed and his hands raised, unaware that everyone around him had sat down."[3]

Another writer recently wrote that he is convinced that he will bow and kneel and raise his hands to the Lord in heaven, and said, "I do not want to wait until I get there to start expressing my adoration and reverence in those ways."[4] He also states that:

> Lifting hands to the Lord in prayer and in praise is not a new phenomenon developed by the Pentecostals . . . Raising hands to the Lord is thoroughly biblical, having been practiced in the worship patterns of the Old Testament period, and carried on into the New Testament era—and therefore into the Christian era.[5]

This same writer contends that churches must learn how to worship God in such Scriptural fashions as lifting hands and that "leaders must model these biblical practices if people are going to learn how and if they are going to overcome their fear."[6] He goes on to suggest that God may even prefer worship with raised hands. He says,

> . . . the important questions are not: what will make me feel comfortable, what fits my traditions, or what will meet my needs? Rather, the important questions are: What kind of worship does God call for? What kind of worship pleases Him? What does Scripture say about what the Lord wants? God wants whole-

hearted worship, and it is reasonable to expect that He wants our bodies as well as our minds.[7]

He then attempts to persuade his readers to raise their hands in worship even if they are not inclined to do so. He says,

Psychologists assure us that our physical actions affect our emotions far more than our emotions affect our actions. We can seldom will ourselves to feel a certain way, but we can will ourselves to act a certain way, and those repeated actions can change our feelings. In other words, if some of us wait for our emotions to prompt us to say 'amen,' or to kneel or lift our hands in worship, we may never do any of them. However, if we simply do what is biblical, even if we do not feel like it at first, in time our emotional response to those behaviors will likely be positive.[8]

Why do some in churches of Christ seem to be aggressively promoting this posture? Most would probably suggest that it is the result of a renewed determination to praise God in Bible ways and manners. The timing of their calls, however, raises a reasonable doubt as to whether this explanation of its popularity is the best explanation. In other words, it is difficult to believe that its popularity in churches of Christ is strictly the result of a renewed determination to praise God in Bible ways and manners when this posture just happens to be one of the "hottest" worship trends in the larger evangelical community. The fact that raising hands in worship is currently one of the fastest growing trends in American "Christianity" suggests that the *primary* reason it is gaining popularity in churches of Christ is that it is fashionable.

Of course, this is not to suggest that there is no Biblical basis for this posture. It is true that in Old Testament times God's people often made supplication with their hands extended toward the temple (Psalm 28:2; 134:2) or toward heaven (1 Kings 8:22; Lamentations 3:41). It is also true that such a posture for prayer seems to have been practiced in New Testament times (1 Timothy 2:8).

The question we must ask is, "What was the significance of this posture in both Old and New Testament times?" Was it a physical way of expressing a deep desire to be with God, much in the same way that a small child wanting to be held raises his hands and arms to an adult? Some have suggested this as an explanation, but there seems to be little hard evidence to support this view.

There seems to be stronger evidence that lifting one's hands in prayer in ancient times may have been symbolic of proclaiming covenant loyalty. A relief which was carved about the time of Hezekiah[9] shows Merodach-Baladan, the Babylonian ruler, making a grant to an official. Each is holding a staff in his left hand while the right hand is raised toward one another in oath.[10] Janice and Richard Leonard state that such traditions as this "no doubt underlie the common practice of lifting hands in worship."[11]

This brief insight into the Biblical practice of lifting hands leads us to conclude that, while lifting hands may have symbolized an important inner reality—a covenant relationship with God—it was never intended by God to be a mandatory or preferred act, gesture, or posture of prayer or praise. Of course, some may claim that Paul's statement that "men in every place . . . pray, lifting up holy hands . . ." (1 Timothy 2:8) implies that it is a preferred posture of prayer. The Spirit's instruction, however, does not demand that one assume a particular physical posture when praying. Instead, He is demanding that those who pray in the assembly possess a particular character of life—one that is consistent with claims of holiness. The emphasis in this verse should not be on "lifting up hands" but on the word "holy." It should be read, ". . . lifting up *holy* hands, . . ."

It should also be pointed out that while proponents of lifting hands appeal to Biblical examples to support the practice, in reality there seems to be some difference between the ancient, Biblical manner of lifting hands and the contemporary manner. As already noted, Biblical references suggest that hands were raised with palms extended toward the temple or heaven to symbolize, at least in part, covenant loyalty.

In the contemporary manner, however, lifting hands can appropriately be described, as some have, as "hand-waving," since many who lift their hands and arms tend to sway them as they do so. In addition, sometimes the worshiper's palms may be upward—toward heaven—in their orientation; at other times they may be turned inward toward each other, and at still other times they may have a downward orientation—toward the floor.

This apparent difference, slight though it may appear, would seem to challenge, at least in part, the contention that "lifting hands to the Lord in prayer and in praise is not a new phenomenon developed by the Pentecostals. . . ."[12] While lifting hands in worship is certainly a Biblical concept, the *manner* in which it is generally practiced in contemporary Christianity does seem to have a distinct pentecostal flavor.

How should congregations respond to this trend? First of all, they should stress that there is nothing inherently wrong with the posture of lifting hands; it is a thoroughly Biblical posture for prayer. They should equally stress, however, that there is nothing inherently preferable about this posture. While Scripture is filled with examples of people worshiping in various physical postures (Daniel 6:10; Luke 22:41; Psalm 95:6; 1 Kings 8:54; 18:42; 1 Samuel 1:26; Matthew 6:5; Genesis 24:26, 48; Luke 18:11,13; 1 Kings 8:22; Nehemiah 8:6; Joshua 7:6-10), never does it suggest that one is preferable to another. Therefore, worshipers may bow their heads, kneel down, raise their hands, sit, stand, lie face down, or assume almost any other physical position one can think of while praying. It simply does not matter what physical posture one assumes while worshiping as long as his disposition of mind and character of life are in harmony with God's will.

The fact, however, that physical posture seems to be of little interest to God does not necessarily mean that it would be appropriate to promote the adoption of any physical posture in every public service. With this in mind, I would suggest that sufficient reason exists to discourage the promotion of lifting hands in the traditional charismatic manner in the public services of most churches of Christ.

Being well aware of the danger of making "flood-gate" arguments, I must admit that one objection I have to promoting the adoption of raising hands is that the adoption of one element of charismatic worship largely because it is fashionable will likely lead to the adoption of others that become fashionable. And since many elements of charismatic worship are closely tied to charismatic doctrine (e.g., being slain in the spirit, glossolalia, and "miracle" healings), there is a real possibly that the adoption of traditional charismatic behavior may eventually lead to an adoption of traditional charismatic doctrine.

Another reason I would discourage promoting the adoption of hand raising is to avoid identification with the charismatic movement. This may at first sound like the extreme "if-our-religious-neighbors-come-in-the-front-door-we-need-to-go-in-the-back" mentality, but such a mentality is certainly not being advocated. What is being suggested is that identification with the charismatic movement—a movement whose legacy has included, as one observed, "confusion and mushy thinking"[13]—is not something to be desired.

This estimate of the charismatic movement is certainly *not* based on a belief that there are no commendable qualities in devout charismatics. Instead, it is simply based on the conviction that basic charismatic theology is unbiblical.[14] I am confident that most who really understand the basic theology of the charismatic movement would agree.

One might ask, "How would hand raising identify one with the charismatic movement?" While there are certainly some doctrinal beliefs and practices that charismatics and non-charismatics share, there are others that have traditionally been so uniquely associated with charismatics that non-charismatics' adoption of them would immediately create an identification with them. Hand raising in public worship is one such practice.

One might be tempted to retort, "Does this mean that since charismatic services are typically characterized by strong emotional displays, we ought to be stoic, cold, life-less, and mechanical in our services?" Of course not. Truth *must* be responded to emotionally. Of course we must, as John MacArthur notes, "first apprehend it with our under-standing and submit to it with our will."[15] So, it is neither emotion nor emotional responses to truth *per se* that are being cautioned against here. What is being cautioned against is simply the embracing of those historically unique physical responses (e.g., hand raising, glossolalia, being slain in the spirit, "holy hilarity," etc.) that would lead one to the logical conclusion that a close association exists with those who practice such things.

Yet another objection I have to promoting the adoption of hand raising is that the promotion of it has the potential of disrupting harmony in the church, and hand raising is sim-ply not worth the price of a disrupted church. Christians must pursue things which make for peace (Romans 14:19). The principle of love for one another must not only govern every decision individual Christians make (Romans 14:5), but also every decision church leaders make.

In light of the possibility of disrupting church harmony, any suggestion that church leaders initiate the practice of lifting hands in their congregations despite the risk of caus-ing criticism and conflict must be challenged. Just as the work of God must never be torn down for the sake of food (Romans 14:20), it must never be torn down for the sake of introducing a trendy posture in the public services. As Howard Norton points out:

> The public worship assembly is critical to our unity as a brotherhood. It always has been. Because of this we must be exceedingly careful when we tamper with it in any way. We are very resilient in churches of Christ when the issues on which we disagree fall

outside the public assembly of the saints. When controversial practices enter the public assembly, however, everyone is affected; and the possibility for division and shattering is scary.[16]

If proponents of charismatic styled hand raising wish to assume such a posture in their private worship or when they worship with others who favor the posture, well and good; but they should rethink insisting that it is their "right" to introduce it into the public assembly if congregational tension and the possibility of division will be generated by its adoption. To create tension by "forcing" hand raising on congregations when it is not necessary would seem to challenge the Spirit's instruction to "walk after love" (cf. Ephesians 5:2; Romans 14:15).

Questions to Guide Study

1. Why do you think more people in churches of Christ are endorsing the practice of raising hands in worship? Do you think its popularity in churches of Christ has any thing to do with its popularity in the wider "Christian" community? Why or why not?

2. What seems to be the historical background for raising hands in prayer during Old and New Testament times?

3. Do you think God prefers one physical posture for worship over another? Why or why not?

4. What are some reasons you would support or discourage raising hands in the public services of churches of Christ?

5. Do you think there are any differences between the manner of hand raising in worship today and hand raising in Bible times? If so, what are some of the differences?

Endnotes

[1]Peter Jennings, *In the Name of God*, ABC News Special Report, aired 17 March, 1995.

[2]Jeff Nelson, "Holding Hands With God: The Senses of Worship—Part 1," in the feature section "Improving Our Worship," *Wineskins* 1 (September 1992): 16.

[3]Ibid.

[4]Dan Dozier, *Come Let Us Adore Him* (Joplin, MO: College Press, 1994), 291.

[5]Ibid., 290.

[6]Ibid., 296.

[7]Ibid., 294.

[8]Ibid., 295.

[9]Hezekiah came to the throne of Judah as a co-regent in 728 B.C. After Ahaz, his father, died in 715 B.C., Hezekiah reigned twenty-nine years until 686 B.C.

[10]James B. Pritchard, *The Ancient Near East* (Princeton: Princeton University Press, 1958), plate 125.

[11]Janice and Richard Leonard, "Symbolism in Biblical Worship," in *The Biblical Foundations of Christian Worship*, The Complete Library of Christian Worship Series, ed. Robert E. Webber, vol. 1 (Nashville, TN: Star Song Publishing, 1993), 40.

[12]See endnote 5.

[13]John MacArthur, Jr. *Charismatic Chaos* (Grand Rapids: Zondervan, 1992): statement on back cover.

[14]For a good analysis of the doctrinal differences between charismatics and non-charismatics see MacArthur's *Charismatic Chaos*.

[15]Ibid., 41.

[16]Howard Norton, "Editor Warns to Be Careful With the Worship Assembly," *Christian Chronicle*, January 1993, C-16.

Chapter 9
"Special" Music

Another significant point of controversy within our fellowship in recent years has pertained to the use of "special music"—solos, trios, quartets, and choirs—in the public worship assembly. Of course, as most readers know, for at least the last half century most churches of Christ have limited their "musical format"[1] in public worship almost exclusively to "congregational singing" (i.e., everyone singing together). In the last decade or so, however, there has been a significant rise in the number of people calling for the use of different musical formats in our public services.

For instance, one writer strongly contends that churches must utilize various musical formats in order to "connect" with a culture that consists of "watchers and listeners, but not participants."[2] He even goes so far as to argue that Scripture actually *commands* the use of musical formats such as solos, choirs, and quartets. He states, "Rather than *forbidding* singing groups in worship, Scripture actually *enjoins them*."[3] He also contends that instead of commanding Christians all to sing at one time (i.e., congregational singing), "Scripture actually says the opposite."[4] He says, "Ephesians 5 actually says that (at least some of the time) *one group of people sings while another group listens.*"[5] He goes on to make such statements as, "In 1 Corinthians 14:26, I found something else that I had not included in my old sermons on worship in assemblies: *solos;*"[6] and "In Scripture, congregational singing is augmented with presentations by solos or singing groups."[7]

Another strong proponent of "special music" in the public worship assembly says concerning 1 Corinthians 14:26, "Here, the individual has composed a 'hymn' or 'solo' (or it is Spirit-inspired) and sings it at worship."[8] He further argues, "If a psalm or hymn can be read by one person while the congregation listens, then a psalm or hymn can be sung by one person while the congregation listens. Musical intonations do not alter anything, theologically or spiritually."[9] He then summarizes this thought by saying, "If you can say it, you can sing it."[10]

Opponents of "special music" in public worship have been just as vocal. One of the strongest opponents of the practice objects to it on grammatical grounds. He argues that an analysis of the construction of Ephesians 5:19 and Colossians 3:16 demands that as the church sings in the public assembly, it must sing together. Of course, he points out that this does not mean that every member must sing the same words at the same time. He notes, "The entire congregation can sing together without each individual singing the same words at the same time."[11]

After long and careful consideration of the pertinent passages, as well as the arguments offered by both proponents and opponents of "special music," I am afraid that the matter simply is not as clear as we might wish. Despite some ambiguity, I must strongly reject the practice; but because of it I cannot dogmatically say, "Solos and other musical formats clearly violate Biblical teaching and are therefore absolutely and unequivocally wrong."

Some of you may be thinking, "How can you reject solos, quartets, and choirs in the public worship assembly if, as some contend, 'Scripture actually *enjoins them*'"[12] (i.e., commands them)? Or "How can you reject choirs or quartets when, as some insist, 'Ephesians 5 actually says that . . . *one group of people sings while another group listens.*'?"[13] And some of you may be thinking, "How can you reject solos when, as some argue, 1 Corinthians 14:26 actually shows an individual singing a solo during the public assembly?"[14]

It is because these passages clearly are *not* saying what some are contending. For instance, Ephesians 5:19 does not "actually say that . . . *one group of people sings while another group listens.*" Instead, it says, "speaking to one another in psalms, hymns, and spiritual songs, singing and making melody with your heart to the Lord."

Similarly, Colossians 3:16 does not *"actually enjoin"* (i.e., command) musical formats such as solos and choirs. Instead, it says, "Let the word of Christ richly dwell within you, with all wisdom teaching and admonishing one another with psalms and hymns and spiritual songs, singing with thankfulness in your hearts to God."

Finally, 1 Corinthians 14:26 does *not* actually show a person singing a solo to the public assembly. Instead, it simply says, "When you assemble, *each one has a psalm*, has a teaching, has a revelation, has a tongue, has an interpretation. . . ." It *may* reflect the idea of solos, but it *may not*. As many have pointed out, there are other legitimate ways to interpret the ambiguous phrase "each one has a psalm."

It may refer to the idea of different people coming to the assembly prepared to "lead" the church in singing a song. Or it may refer to people bringing self-composed or Spirit-inspired songs to the assembly with the intent of teaching them to the church. It may even refer to a composition which is written in the style of the Psalter[15] and brought to the assembly to be read, not sung.[16]

Even if the word *psalmos* in 1 Corinthians 14:26 does refer to a song as opposed to a style of writing, which seems to be the case, the term itself does not indicate under what circumstances it is to be sung.[17] As one writer has said, while the phrase "each one has a psalm" may reflect individuals composing psalms and bringing them to the assembly, "no justification exists contextually or linguistically for assuming only individuals would sing the psalm to the exclusion of the entire assembly."[18] To say it another way, although the phrase probably "refers to an individual who has, by inspiration, composed a suitable worship song," it "says nothing about the subsequent singing of that song."[19]

It should also be added that many proponents of solos, choirs, and similar musical formats point out the strong possibility that the earliest forms of singing in Christian assemblies were "responsorial" and "antiphonal" rather than "congregational." Responsorial singing occurs when one person or group sings a text and another person or group responds with a refrain. Antiphonal singing has people or groups singing in alternating parts. Many proponents of "special music" seem to be suggesting that the likelihood of these forms being used in early Christian assemblies lends support to their view.

Even if it is true that the earliest forms of "church music" were responsorial and antiphonal, I fail to see how this fact supports the idea of soloists and choirs. Although these forms of music may not be strictly classified as "congregational," it seems clear that the entire congregation functioned as active participants in both the responsorial and antiphonal format. Therefore, if anything, historical data seems to argue for full congregational participation in praising God in song.

To summarize, the New Testament does not *command* solos, duets, trios, quartets, or choirs in the public assembly. Nowhere does it *say* that one group of people sings while another group listens. And nowhere does it *clearly show* that "congregational singing is augmented with presentations by solos or singing groups." If the New Testament really did any of these things, there would be no controversy on the subject. If churches depicted in the New Testament really did any of these things, how could there be any controversy on the matter?

Although there is *no* clear New Testament precedent for the use of "special music" in the public worship assembly, I do not feel that it can be said that "solos and other musical formats in the public assembly clearly violate Biblical teaching and are therefore absolutely and unequivocally wrong." Here is why.

In 1 Corinthians 14:26 Paul establishes the following principle to "regulate" what occurs during a Christian worship assembly: "Let all things be done for edification." Since he argues in verses 1-19 of the same chapter that edification is possible only when spiritual ideas and concepts are conveyed through understandable words, it seems clear that his exhortation, "Let all things be done for edification," restricts the activities of a Christian worship assembly only to those activities which can convey spiritual ideas and concepts through words which people can understand. The fact that he stops the brethren at Corinth from utilizing "tongue speakers" in their assemblies when there was no one present to interpret (v. 28) seems to offer clear support to this conclusion.

With this in mind, who can deny that a person standing in front of the assembly and singing is conveying spiritual ideas and concepts through words which people can understand? In other words, it does not seem to violate the principle, "Let all things be done for edification." Because of this principle, the suggestion that "if you can say it, you can sing it" does seem to have some validity. In other words, because of this principle, I would have a very difficult time explaining how a person can stand before an assembly and say or read something that is Biblical, but strongly challenge him if he stands before an assembly and sings the exact same words to a simple, reverent melody.

Before leaving the suggestion that solos and other musical formats *may* be permissible in the public assembly, something else needs to be said. If a church chooses to utilize a soloist on occasion to stand before the assembly and instruct, exhort, and admonish those present, then 1 Timothy 2:12 seems to make it very clear that the soloist *must* be a man. After all, if a soloist is essentially functioning as a teacher, and he is, then that person must meet the criteria imposed on the church by the Holy Spirit regarding teaching. In other words, if it is true that "if you can say it to the congregation when it is assembled, you can sing it to them," then those who "sing it" to the assembly must be permitted by God to "say it" to the assembly.

Despite the *possibility* that a *male* soloist, or a quartet of *men*, *may* be able to stand before a Christian worship assembly and sing without violating clear Biblical teaching or a clear Biblical principle, I strongly reject the use of such "special music" in public worship for several reasons.

First of all, the use of soloists, quartets, choirs, and similar musical formats reduces a congregation's active participation in the worship service. As suggested earlier, changes in public worship that will increase a congregation's active participation in the service should be encouraged, but changes that will reduce their active participation in it, should not.

Of course, this is not to suggest that a person is *not* participating in worship if he is only listening. It is simply noting that actively participating in the singing of praises to God is a different kind of participation than merely listening to praises being sung; and this kind of participation must be encouraged and preserved.

Twenty-first century American culture may largely be a culture of "watchers and listeners, but not participants," but that does not mean the church should jettison from its public service those elements that encourage a person's active participation. Christians need to participate actively in public worship. Congregational singing encourages active participation while "special music" does not.

Another objection I have to "special music" is that it is designed—at least in contemporary American Evangelicalism—to provide *some* entertainment value to the congregation; and as argued in earlier chapters, churches must resist the temptation to start forcing their public worship assemblies into an entertainment format.

Some may protest the suggestion that the use of "special music" is intended, at least in part, to provide an audience with a measure of entertainment. The fact, however, that a person with a less than stellar voice is not usually solicited to sing seems to make this suggestion difficult to argue against. If the real intent of utilizing a solo in an assembly is simply to convey information that will teach, admonish, and exhort those present, why should the quality of the soloist's voice really matter? And yet it does—at least, as just noted, it does in modern evangelical churches.

As noted earlier, one writer suggested that "special music" will "connect" with the modern culture in a way that congregational singing cannot. Of course it will. Why? Because there is an entertainment design to it. As suggested earlier, many modern worshipers are addicted to entertainment. They have been raised in an overly-stimulated culture, and therefore they believe that entertainment should be the representation of all experience, even worship. So, when entertainment elements are brought into the public worship assembly, many modern worshipers will naturally "connect" with them.

This fact is, however, no reason for the church to adopt entertainment elements for its public services. Instead, as also noted earlier, churches need charitably and patiently to call modern worshipers to examine their attitudes toward worship; then they should teach them what it really means to worship God.

A final objection to adopting "special music" is that, like lifting hands in traditional charismatic fashion, it has the potential of disrupting harmony in the church, and an occasional solo is not worth the price of a disrupted church. As noted earlier, when controversial practices are brought into the public worship assembly of a church, everyone is affected. Consequently, the probability for division in that church soars high.

Christians must pursue things which make for peace (Romans 14:19). The principle of love for one another must govern not only every decision individual Christians make (Romans 14:5), but also every decision church leaders make. With this criterion, why would anyone want to introduce something into the public worship that so many people strongly oppose?

Some may argue that it is necessary to adopt "special music" if the church hopes to evangelize the modern generation to the fullest possible extent; therefore, opposition to "special music" *must* be challenged and overcome. Does anyone really believe this? Does anyone actually believe that those who are *really* disposed to eternal life are going to turn away from Christ simply because there is not an occasional solo in a Christian worship assembly? In other words, are they going to turn away because Christian worship is not framed as entertainment? I would suggest that those who turn away from Christ because there is not a regular soloist or quartet in the assembly are more disposed to self-fulfillment than to eternal life.

Questions to Guide Study

1. Read Ephesians 5:19, Colossians 3:16, and 1 Corinthians 14:26. Is there a clear command in these passages for the church to use solos, choirs, quartets, etc. when it gathers for worship? Support your answer.

2. Read 1 Corinthians 14:26 again. Does this verse clearly show the utilization of solos in a public worship context? What are other valid ways to understand the phrase "each one has a psalm" other than understanding it to mean a person is singing a solo?

3. What are some reasons that you would support or reject the use of "special music" in public worship?

4. Why do you think more and more people in churches of Christ are promoting the use of "special music" in their public services?

Endnotes

[1] "Musical format" is a term Lynn Anderson uses to mean "style of presentation." He says, "Musical format is the way in which we present the music, including 'presentational' music . . . and 'participatory' music . . . Other formats include such a variety as congregational singing . . . , antiphonal singing . . . , choral music . . . , and solos" (Lynn Anderson, "Music That Makes Sense," *Wineskins* 1/9 (January/February 1993): 27).

[2] Lynn Anderson, "Music That Makes Sense," *Wineskins* 1/9 (January/February 1993): 30.

[3] Ibid., 28.

[4] Ibid.

[5] Ibid.

[6] Ibid., Here he is specifically referring to Paul's observation, "When you assemble, *each one has a psalm*, has a teaching, has a revelation, has a tongue, has an interpretation. . . ."

[7] Ibid., 28-29.

[8] Calvin Warpula, "Special Music? Yes," *Image* 8/2 (March/April 1992): 19.

[9] Ibid., 27.

[10] Ibid.

[11] Dave Miller, *Piloting the Strait: A Guidebook for Assessing Change in Churches of Christ* (Pulaski, TN: Sain Publications, 1996), 209-210. Brother Miller's analysis of the construction of these passages can be found in his book *Singing and New Testament Worship*. Abilene, TX: Quality Publishing, 1994.

[12] See endnote 3.

[13] See endnote 5.

[14] See endnote 6.

[15] Gerhard Delling, "humnos" in *Theological Dictionary of the New Testament*, vol. 8 (Grand Rapids: Eerdmans Publishing Co., 1972), 499 (note 73), 500.

[16]Vincent insists that the use of a psalm is "not restricted to singing" (Marvin R. Vincent, *Word Studies in the New Testament*, vol 3 (New York, NY: Charles Scribner's Sons, 1906), 507.).

[17]K.H. Bartels, "Psalmos" in Colin Brown, ed. *The New International Dictionary of New Testament Theology*, vol. 3 (Grand Rapids: Zondervan Publishing House, 1978), 671-672.

[18]Miller, 206.

[19]Ibid.

Section Three
Christian Worship

Chapter 10
Praise God For Worship!

I have suggested several times that the only real way to counteract the modern generation's desire to pour worship into an entertainment format is to teach them—charitably, carefully, and thoroughly—what it really means to worship the living God. Consequently, it would seem incomplete to end this book without discussing the true meaning of Christian worship.

Worship Is About God

Through countless examples of and references to worship, Scripture clearly shows that the meaning and purpose of worship is to give honor and praise to God. Worship is, as Michael Weed says, "essentially doxology."[1] All creatures in heaven and on the earth are called on to praise God. The Psalmist exhorts, "Praise the Lord! Praise the Lord from the heavens; Praise Him in the heights! Praise Him, all His angels; Praise Him, all His hosts! Praise Him, sun and moon; Praise Him, all stars of light! Praise Him, highest heavens, and the waters that are above the heavens!" (Psalm 148:1-4). "Let heaven and earth praise Him, the seas and everything that moves in them" (Psalm 69:34). "Let everything that has breath praise the Lord. Praise the Lord!" (Psalm 150:6).

What are the implications of the statement, *The meaning and purpose of worship is to give honor and praise to God?* Perhaps the most important implication is that, as many have observed, worship is primarily about God, not man; or as others have noted, worship is God-centered, not man-centered. What exactly does it mean to say that worship is about God, not man, and that worship is God-centered, not man-centered?

For one thing, it means that a person's *primary* reason for worshiping should be to give glory, laud, and honor to God. On the other hand, it means that a person's primary reason for worshiping should *not* be to get personal rewards or achieve personal goals—no matter how worthy or desirable a goal may seem. For the benefit of many modern worshipers, it means that a person's primary reason for worshiping must not be to receive emotional stimulation or be entertained. It also means that the value of worship must never be measured by the amount of emotional stimulation or level of entertainment that a service provides.

To worship primarily in order to get a personal payoff or to measure worship primarily on the basis of what happens to a worshiper emotionally makes man, not God, the center of worship. Weed says it this way: "However much God is mentioned, worship becomes human- and self-centered, not God-centered, when its focus becomes the experience of the worshiper rather than the praise and adoration of the one being worshiped."[2]

What happens to worship when man places himself at the center of it? If worship by its very nature is God-centered, and it is, then the moment it becomes man-centered is the moment that it ceases to be true worship.

Of course, as I emphasized earlier, this doesn't mean that emotional uplift from worship is bad or undesirable. If one is emotionally stimulated from worship, well and good. In fact, emotional upheaval or uplift often accompanies worship. What I am saying is simply that, in the end, after a person has worshiped, the consideration that matters most is, "Was God praised, and was His magnificence declared?"

Nor does this emphasis mean that it is inappropriate to desire personal blessings from worship. God has designed worship so that true worshipers will receive many spiritual blessings from the occasion. Since this is the case, surely it cannot be wrong to enter worship with an expectation and desire to receive those blessings.

What I am saying is that, as far as motives for worship go, there are right and wrong priorities; and when praising and honoring God are not the top priorities in worship, worship is corrupted because its true meaning and purpose have been perverted. What I am saying is that when seeking personal payoffs—even legitimate ones—becomes as important as or more important than, praising and honoring God, a person needs to reorder his motives for worshiping.

Since the true purpose of worship is to give honor and praise to God, worshipers must view worship, not as a means to an end, but as an end in itself. They must not think that the true function of worship is to create a euphoric emotional state within people—although true worship *may*, and often does, produce emotional uplift in people. They must not think that the true function of worship is to effect a behavioral change in people—although true worship *may*, and often does, effect a behavioral change in people. They must not think that the true function of worship is to make Christianity attractive to the unchurched world—although true worship *may*, and often does, inspire some people to examine the Christian faith more closely. They must not think that the true function of worship is to promote church programs and social agendas—although it *may* be right and proper to mention such activities at times in the public worship assembly. And they must not think that the true function of worship is to fill pews and swell collection plates—although a Biblical, challenging, and inspirational service *may*, and often does, result in more and more people gathering with a congregation to worship.

Although many desirable things may *result* from worship, the primary *purpose* of worship is *not* to bring about these things. The primary *purpose* of worship is to give glory, laud, and honor to God. To worship God primarily for reasons other than this is to corrupt worship by distorting its true meaning and purpose. Not only is there a desperate need for modern worshipers to understand this fundamental truth about worship, but there is also a desperate need for modern churches to understand it as well.

Worship Is a Verb

Another important thing to remember about worship is that, as some have suggested, it is a verb. That is, worship is something a person does. Consequently, it must, by its very nature, involve an expression or action. These expressions of praise and devotion may be visible and audible, or they may be silent in one's own thoughts, but they *must* exist before a person is really worshiping.

The fact that worship involves some act or expression of praise and devotion can be demonstrated simply from an examination of the Hebrew and Greek words most frequently translated "worship" in the English Bible.

The Old Testament word most frequently translated "worship" is *chawah*. It means "to bow down," and in its original sense meant "to prostrate oneself on the ground."[3] Moses "made haste to bow low toward the earth and worship" (Exodus 34:8). Job "fell to the ground and worshiped" (Job 1:20), and the Psalmist exhorts, "Come, let us worship and bow down; let us kneel before the Lord our Maker" (Psalm 95:6).

The word most frequently translated "worship" in the New Testament is *proskuneo*. The Greeks found this word to be the nearest equivalent to *chawah*. It means to "(fall down and) worship, do obeisance to, prostrate oneself before, do reverence to, welcome respectfully."[4]

In addition to these words, other words in Scripture also show that worship involves some sort of action or expression.

For example, *prayer, praise*, and *sacrifice* are all expressions or acts of worship which dominate the pages of Scripture.

Mentioning this aspect of worship may sound elementary and unnecessary to some, but it needs to be mentioned in order to counteract the increasingly popular notion that worship is merely a feeling, attitude, or emotion. One writer, for instance, says:

> Ordinarily it is thought that worship consists of the mechanical acts of singing, praying, giving, expounding God's Word and taking the Lord's Supper. *But these external performances are not worship;* rather they are the outward expression of it. *Worship . . . is an attitude of the soul. It is a subjective experience of the soul* in its adoration of God, *which may find expression in overt forms* (emphasis added).[5]

In response to this view of worship it should first be noted that no biblical passage exists which says, or even implies, that worship is merely an "attitude of the soul." Of course, there are many passages, as we will note later, which teach that one cannot worship God acceptably without the proper "attitude of soul." There is a world of difference, however, between saying that a particular "attitude of the soul" is an essential ingredient of true worship and saying that true worship is *only* "an attitude of the soul."

A second reply to this view is that Scripture demonstrates clearly that worship was something which Old and New Testament saints *did* at specific times and places; it wasn't merely an internal emotion, attitude, or disposition of mind. For instance, Abraham said to his young men, "Stay here with the donkey, and I and the lad will go yonder; and we will worship and return to you" (Genesis 22:1-5). David, after the death of his son, ". . . arose from the ground, washed, anointed himself, and changed his clothes; and he came into the house of the Lord and worshiped. Then he came to his own house . . ." (2 Samuel 12:20). The Ethiopian eunuch "had come to Jerusalem to worship" and "was returning . . ." (Acts 8:27-28). Paul asked the governor to note that "no more than twelve days ago I went up to Jerusalem to worship" (Acts 24:11). Finally, after asking where the newborn messiah was, the magi said, "We . . . have come to worship Him" (Matthew 2:2).

Some may ask, "but didn't all of these people feel something while doing something?" Absolutely, but it was the feeling *and* doing that constituted their worship; it was not just the feeling. While Abraham's, David's, and Paul's attitude of adoration and awe drove them to worship and gave value to their worship, their inward adoration of God was not worship until it was expressed in some way.

This is certainly not to suggest that *true* worship is merely a set of mechanical rituals that one thoughtlessly performs. As we will see later, *true* worship requires *much* more than just an outward expression of homage. What needs to be seen clearly is that for worship to be worship, there *must* be an expression of praise and adoration.

Twenty-four-Hour-a-Day Worship

Another popular notion of worship which needs to be challenged is that "all of one's life is worship," or to say it another way, "everything a Christian does is worship." Some have even said it this way: "A Christian worships twenty-four hours a day." Those who make these assertions usually conclude that, since all of life is worship, "technically, it is not biblical to say we are 'going to worship.'" I must raise several objections to this view.

First of all, as noted in connection with the "worship-is-just-an-attitude" view, no Biblical passage exists which states, or even implies, that everything a Christian does is worship. Of course, there are some passages, like 1 Corinthians 10:31, in which proponents of this view claim to find strong support for their position. This verse exhorts, "Whether, then, you eat or drink or whatever you do, do all to the glory of God."

In connection with this discussion, the one thing that seems obvious about this verse is that it clearly does *not* say, "Everything a Christian does is worship." In fact, worship is not even mentioned in the verse. In this verse, Paul is simply exhorting Christians to live their lives in such a way that God is always honored—even in the most mundane, routine, and seemingly "nonspiritual" activities in life like eating and drinking. Paul just as easily could have said, "Don't do anything that will bring discredit or reproach on God," and his statement would have meant the same thing. It is simply that he chose to use a positive statement, rather than a negative one, to make this exhortation.

Some have also suggested that Romans 12:1 lends strong support to the "all-of-life-is-worship" view. In this verse, Paul exhorts his readers to "present your bodies a living and holy sacrifice," declaring that doing so constitutes one's *logike latreia*.

The supposed support in this verse for the "all-of-life-is-worship" view comes from the fact that some English versions translate *logike latreia* as "spiritual act of worship" (NIV) or as something quite similar. It is easy to understand how some who rely on versions that opt for such a translation may conclude that everything a person does in life is worship. It is important to note, however, that other versions of the English Bible translate *logike latreia* quite differently. For instance, the NKJV translates it "reasonable service."

The reason translators are not in agreement on this matter is that the words *logikos* (from which the word *logike* comes) and *latreuo* (from which the word *latreia* comes) both have a wide lexical range. The word *logikos* can mean either "reasonable/rational" or "spiritual." The English words "logic" and "logical" are derived from this word. The word *latreuo* can mean either "serve" or "worship." It is important to note, however, that "worship" is *not* the general meaning of *latreuo*; it is a more narrow meaning of it. The general meaning of *latreuo* is "serve" (cf. Romans 1:9; Luke 1:74; Acts 24:14).

Since more than one translation of *logike latreia* is grammatically possible, how can one know which translation is better—"spiritual act of worship" or "reasonable service"? In cases such as this, context must make that determination.

I believe the context of Romans 12:1 favors the latter option—"reasonable service." Why? Because "reasonable service" seems to give a better sense to what Paul is trying to say. Consider the context. Paul concludes chapter 11 with the observation that God desires to show all men mercy (v. 32). He then contemplates the mercy of God, becomes overwhelmed, and bursts forth in praise (vv. 33-36). Finally, in the first two verses of chapter 12, he exhorts his readers to give their lives to God. The basis for his exhortation is that when one stops to consider what God has done for him ("in view of God's mercy"), the only *reasonable* or *rational* response is to give one's life ("offer your bodies as living sacrifices") in *service* to God.

Another objection I have to the "all-of-life-is-worship" view is that it destroys worship as a meaningful category. If everything a person does is worship, then when one lifts his voice to God in praise and adoration, categorically that action is no different than when a person is dozing off on the couch while watching his favorite television show, with God not even in his consciousness. Does anyone really believe that a person is worshiping God even when God is not in his or her consciousness?

Of course, some may argue that God should always be in a Christian's consciousness. While this sounds right, and in a figurative sense may be right, in a real, biological sense it is wrong. Not counting the eight or so hours a day that most people are in a state called sleep in which there is little or no conscious thought, human beings by design cannot always be conscious of all they know even when they are awake.

Unlike God, who has a constant consciousness of all things, man can only think about one thing at a time. Of course, the mind processes information so quickly that it often creates the perception that many thoughts are being entertained simultaneously. Because of this limitation, a person actually knows a great deal more than he is conscious of at any one moment. Most things he knows are stored away in "memory banks," so to speak. Insofar as he is able, then, he recalls them to his consciousness when he needs to think about them.

Since in a real, biological sense a person *cannot* always be conscious of God, those who insist that a Christian is worshiping twenty-four hours a day *must* concede that he is worshiping even when God is not in his consciousness. Once this concession is made, logic demands a further concession that "worship" is not a unique, distinct, and identifiable category of life. In statements such as, "technically, it is not biblical to say we are 'going to worship,'" many proponents of the "all-of-life-is-worship" view seem to have reached this very conclusion.

My final objection to the "all-of-life-is-worship" view is that the pattern of Biblical language clearly shows that not all of one's life is worship. On the contrary, it shows that worship is a unique event which has a definite beginning and end and that it is very Biblical to say "We are going to worship." As noted previously, Abraham, David, the eunuch, Paul, and the Magi all *went* somewhere *to* worship—to a mountain, to the house of the Lord, to Jerusalem, and to Bethlehem.

Phrases found in these accounts such as "will go . . . and . . . worship . . ." (Genesis 22:1-5); "came . . . and worshiped" (2 Samuel 12:20); "had come . . . to worship (Acts 8:27-28); "went . . . to worship" (Acts 24:11); and "have come to worship . . ." (Matthew 2:2) seem to make it clear that these worshipers did *not* consider everything they did to be worship. Instead, they obviously believed that there was a moment in time when they would begin worshiping and a moment in time when they would stop worshiping. Before worshiping on the mountain, Abraham told his servants that after he and Isaac had worshiped they would come back to them. After worshiping in the house of the Lord, David returned to his own house. And after worshiping in Jerusalem, the eunuch was returning home.

Why have so many modern worshipers concluded that "all of one's life is worship"? As many have observed, this rather popular notion stems from a confusion of *service* and *worship*.

Many seem to think that these terms are strictly synonymous, but they are not. One writer, for instance, writes regarding Israel, "Their total life was a service (worship) before the Lord."

Although the word *serve* often includes the idea of *worship* (e.g., Joshua 24:15), it does not always mean *worship* exclusively. Unless otherwise determined by context, the word *serve* or *service* describes a *general response* to God. In other words, when a person is said to serve God, the reference is not usually to one specific aspect of his "work" for God—sometimes it is, but not usually. Instead, it is usually referring to the totality of his "work," that is, *everything* which he does for God. The word *worship*, on the other hand, describes a *specific response* to God. In other words, worship is just one specific way that a person serves God.

It is important to realize that a person may serve and bring glory to God in many ways without actually worshiping Him. In other words, it is not proper to assign the term *worship* to every deed that a person does in response to God's will. Some ways that a person may serve God without worshiping Him include being a good employee, a good spouse, a good parent, a good neighbor, living a morally upright life, and being compassionate to the poor.

When a Christian man takes his wife to dinner and a movie, he is serving God, pleasing God, and bringing glory (i.e., honor) to God, but the act of driving to the restaurant is not itself worship. When he plays catch with his children, he is serving God, pleasing God, and bringing glory to God, but the act of throwing a baseball is not itself worship. And when he buys groceries for a shut-in or mows a sick neighbor's yard, he is serving God, pleasing God, and bringing glory to God, but the act of mowing is not itself worship.

Of course, a person may worship while driving to a restaurant, or while playing catch, or while mowing a shut-in's yard. After all, a person may pray and sing praises to God while doing any of these things. In doing so, however, that person is actually simultaneously serving God in different ways. He is serving God by mowing the shut-in's yard, while at the same time he's serving God by worshiping Him.

Harold Shank makes an observation that may help clarify what I am saying. He says, "Clearly the food service in the soup kitchen differs in substantial ways from the worship service on Sunday, but Christians seek to glorify God in both kinds of service."[6] He continues, "We might imagine a theological outline: service to God is a general category, and the different kinds of service are subcategories. One kind of service is worship; another kind is financial giving; still another . . . is our compassion for the weak and poor."

Service
    a. Worship
    b. Giving
    c. Compassion[7]

How do activities like playing catch with one's children or mowing a shut-in's yard or having compassion for the poor glorify God? In the same way that a child's behavior can honor his or her parents. Parents of virtuous and well-behaved children are respected and held in high esteem by others. Why? Because most people realize that a child's attitude and behavior generally reflect the training and character of his parents. Similarly, when a child of God lives a morally excellent life, most people will realize that his character is the direct result of God's influence and guidance. As a result, only honorable things can be said about God.

When Paul challenges Christians to "do all to the glory of God" (1 Corinthians 10:31), he is not telling them to consider everything they do to be worship. He is simply bringing to their consciousness the fact that everything they do reflects on God in one way or another, either honoring God or bringing reproach upon Him; and he is challenging them to be sure that their day-to-day decisions honor God. Paul's point is similar to that of the father who tells his teenage son who is preparing to go out with friends, "Son, please don't dishonor your mother and me tonight."

To summarize, Scripture clearly demonstrates that worship is primarily about God, not man; it is God-centered, not man-centered. Scripture also clearly demonstrates that worship involves an expression or act of homage; it is something that one *consciously does*. While worship has an impact on everything a person does in life, and while everything a Christian does in life is done in service to God and brings glory to Him, not everything a Christian does in life can be classified as worship. Nor is worship simply an attitude. While one's attitude gives value to worship, adoration is not worship until it is expressed. Therefore, some expression of adoration is essential in worship.

Questions to Guide Study

1. What is the meaning and purpose of worship?

2. What Biblical evidence is there, if any, which shows that worship involves an expression or action?

4. Discuss the validity of the following two views of worship: (1) "everything a person does is worship," and (2) "worship is only an attitude."

5. How are "service" and "worship" related, yet different?

6. Consider the following expression: "We are going to worship." Is it correct to say this? Support your answer.

Endnotes

[1]Michael R. Weed, "Worship and Ethics: Confession, Character, Conduct," *Christian Studies* No. 13 (1993): 48.

[2]Ibid, 50.

[3]R. Laird Harris, Gleason L. Archer, Jr., and Bruce K. Waltke, *Theological Wordbook of the Old, Testament* (Chicago: Moody Press, 1980), 267.

[4]Walter Bauer, *A Greek-English Lexicon of the New Testament and Other Early Christian Literature*, 2d ed., rev. William F. Arndt, F. Wilbur Gingrich, and Frederick W. Danker (Chicago: University of Chicago Press, 1979), 716.

[5]Wayman D. Miller, *Worship—A Transcendent Wonder*, as quoted by Dan Dozier in *Come Let Us Adore Him* (College Press 1994), 51.

[6]Harold Shank, "Worship and Ethics," chap. in *In Search of Wonder: A Call to Worship Renewal*, ed. Lynn Anderson (West Monroe, LA: Howard Publishing Co., 1995), 99.

[7]Ibid., 99-100.

Chapter 11
Worship Which Is Worthy

In 1 Timothy 2:1-2 Paul writes, "First of all, then, I urge that entreaties and prayers, petitions and thanksgivings, be made on behalf of all men, for kings and all who are in authority, in order that we may lead a tranquil and quiet life in all godliness and dignity." At least two things can fairly be inferred from this exhortation. First, prayer should occupy a place of primary importance in the life of the church. Second, prayer should *not* be confined to one's own narrow interests.

Paul follows this exhortation with the observation, "This is good and acceptable in the sight of God our Savior . . ." (v. 3). Commenting on verse 3 Donald Guthrie contends, "The two parts of this verse should be taken separately: (a) universal prayer is *good*; (b) it is *acceptable in the sight of God*."[1] Guthrie then suggests, "This latter proposition presents the ultimate standard for all Christian worship."[2]

I agree with Guthrie's suggestion. The question, "Is it acceptable to God?" must be the ultimate standard by which all individuals and churches measure and evaluate their worship. Why? Simply put, because Scripture clearly shows that: (1) God has *never* accepted just any worship (Genesis

4:1-5); and (2) when people worshiped God unacceptably, they were punished (Leviticus. 10:1-2; Isaiah 1:10-20; Amos 5:21-27).

What are the implications of the fact that "acceptability to God" must be the ultimate standard by which all Christian worship is measured? First of all, it means that no Christian should ever be content with the fact that he is merely a worshiper of the one true God. Instead, he should always be vigilant to make whatever adjustments are necessary in his life, beliefs, and/or worship practices to ensure that his worship is *acceptable* to the one true God. Christians must remember that God is seeking "*true* worshipers," not just "worshipers" (John 4:23).

It also means that any other standard that is being used as the primary standard for measuring worship must be thrown out—or at least subordinated to the "acceptability to God" standard. With this in mind, two standards that many modern worshipers and churches seem to be using as their primary standard for measuring worship are "favorable public opinion" (i.e., "does the general public find the public services appealing?") and "personal enjoyment" (i.e., "do the public services generate an exciting emotional experience?").

If this is true—and it would seem difficult to argue that it is not—then one of the most desperate needs in Christendom today is for people to be taught that whether or not a worship service is appealing to the general public has no real bearing on whether or not God accepts that worship. Likewise, they need to be taught that, although worship often results in emotional stimulation, whether or not a service generates an exciting emotional experience has no real bearing on whether or not God accepts that worship. In other words, a worship service may have great appeal to the general public or be very emotionally stimulating and yet be unacceptable to God. Helping people come to a realization and appreciation of these facts should go a long way toward stopping them from measuring worship primarily against these and other inappropriate standards.

What Constitutes Acceptable Worship?

To assert that all Christian worship must be measured against the question, "Is it acceptable to God?" evokes the question: "What exactly constitutes acceptable worship?" Where worship is concerned, has God left man to wonder what He will and will not accept? In other words, has man been relegated to worship as he deems appropriate and then hope without any real assurance that God will accept what he offers? Certainly not.

Jesus never would have said that God is seeking "true worshipers" (John 4:23) and then failed to reveal to man what makes worship "true." If He had done this, it seems fair to say that it would have been a cruel trick to play on mankind; and as some have observed, God does not play cruel tricks on people. Throughout human history, any time God placed a demand on people, He always told them exactly how to meet that demand.

With this fact firmly in mind, it is important to note that the exclusive means through which God makes demands on people today and tells them how to meet those demands is the written word. The Scriptures contain all the information necessary for a person to become everything that God wants him to be (2 Timothy 3:16-17). In other words, the Scripture contains all the information necessary for a person to become acceptable to God in every sphere and circumstance of life. And since being a true worshiper is part of what God seeks in each person (John 4:23), logic dictates that within Scripture God has revealed exactly what makes worship "true."

Given today's religious climate, it seems necessary to elaborate on this point a bit further before discussing what exactly constitutes acceptable worship. There is a tendency today for many professing Christians to put more trust in their own intuition than in Scripture when it comes to determining how to meet God's expectations—especially in the sphere of worship. Those who are disposed to this tendency need to be reminded, however, that intuition is *not* a reliable compass in *any* spiritual matter—including worship.

The very existence of the Bible proves this fact. If people were capable of determining intuitively what God would and would not accept, why would God bring Scripture into being? What purpose would it possibly serve? And if people were capable of determining intuitively what God would and would not accept, why would God call people to read Scripture, study it, embrace its teaching, and preach it? (Acts 17:1-2; 2 Timothy 2:15; Colossians 3:16; 2 Timothy 4:2).

The fact is, the Bible exists because man *cannot* know intuitively what is and is not acceptable to God in spiritual matters such as worship. Man needs some objective source of perfect information which exists outside himself to know these things; and that objective, perfect, outside source of information is Scripture. To sum it up, the Bible is the *only* "sure thing" that man has to "go on" in spiritual matters such as worship. Consequently, those who choose to rely on the subjective and imperfect information that intuition supplies are destined to fall short of God's expectations in many spiritual matters—including, but certainly not limited to, worship.

Convinced that only Scripture contains the answer to the question, "What constitutes acceptable worship?" I would suggest that the Bible identifies six fundamental principles of acceptable worship. In other words, acceptable worship has six basic ingredients. Of course, there is no single verse in Scripture which lists these principles in some legal format. Like acquiring the Biblical teaching on any spiritual matter, the suggestion that there are six fundamental principles of acceptable worship comes from a careful combination and comparison of all the Biblical facts concerning and relating to worship.

I would further suggest that the basic principles of acceptable worship have never changed throughout human history. The same thing that made Abel's worship acceptable to God made Abraham's worship acceptable to God. The same thing that made Abraham's worship acceptable to God made Moses' worship acceptable to God. And the same thing that made Moses' worship acceptable to God made Paul's worship acceptable to God. In other words, the things that made worship by Old Testament saints acceptable to God are the same things that make worship by New Testament saints acceptable to God. On the other hand, the things that made worship by those who lived under the Old Testament system *un*acceptable to God are the same things that make worship by those who live under the New Testament system *un*acceptable to God. What are these six fundamental principles, or ingredients, of acceptable worship? The remainder of this chapter will attempt to answer this question.

No Other Gods

The first principle of acceptable worship is that God must be the exclusive object of one's worship. God refuses to share devotion with anyone or anything. His very first written directive to Israel was, "You shall have no other gods before Me. You shall not make for yourself an idol, or any likeness of what is in heaven above or on the earth beneath or in the water under the earth. You shall not worship them or serve them; for I, the Lord your God, am a jealous God . . ." (Exodus 20:3-5a). Centuries later Christ basically restated this principle when He said to Satan, "Begone Satan! For it is written, 'You shall worship the Lord your God, and serve Him only'" (Matthew 4:8-10).

This principle was also taught when John fell at an angel's feet to worship. The angel responded by saying, "Do not do that; I am a fellow servant of yours and of your brethren the prophets and of those who heed the words of this book; worship God" (Revelation 22:9). Still another example which shows that worship is to be reserved exclusively for God is found in Acts 10. When Peter entered Cornelius' house, the text says Cornelius fell at Peter's feet "and worshiped him."[3] The text goes on to say, however, that Peter "raised him up, saying, 'Stand up; I too am just a man.'" (vv. 25-26).

Why does God refuse to share reverence with anyone or anything? Simply put, because nothing or no one is like God. As Jack Cottrell says, the fact of creation points out that reality is divided "into two qualitatively distinct categories: the Creator and the created."[4] All things in the latter category are naturally subordinate in nature to those things in the former. Since God alone exists in the former category, all things are subordinate in nature to Him. Only God is transcendent, eternal, and infinite Creator; all else is finite and transitory creation. Because of this fact, nothing or no one is worthy of worship except God.

Throughout history, those who split their allegiance between pagan gods and the one true God have suffered divine consequences. For instance, in the eighth century B.C. God delivered a message to Israel through the prophet Amos. He asked them, "Did you present Me with sacrifices and grain offerings in the wilderness for forty years, O house of Israel?" (Amos 5:25). Although scholars are divided as to whether Amos expected a positive or negative answer to this question, he probably anticipated a "yes."

God then says, "You also carried along Sikkuth your king and Kiyyun, your images, the star of your gods which you made for yourselves" (Amos 5:26). During the forty years of wilderness wandering Israel did bring sacrifices to God, but these sacrifices were often unacceptable because the Israelites were also worshiping idols.

Why did God call Israel to remember the idolatry that their ancestors had committed several centuries earlier? Because the idolatry which began in the wilderness had continued to Amos' day. Those in Amos' day were doing the same thing that their wilderness-wandering ancestors had done. As a result, God told them, "Therefore, I will make you go into exile beyond Damascus . . ." (Amos 5:27). In the New Testament Stephen identifies the specific location of their exile as Babylon (Acts 7:43).

When it comes to God's rejection of worship today because of idolatry, few professing Christians probably feel that this is a real possibility since they are convinced that they would never worship an idol. I am convinced, however, that such confidence reflects a less than full understanding of idolatry and that committing idolatry is an ever-present threat against which we all must constantly be on guard.

If asked, most people today would probably explain idolatry as the act of ascribing honor and praise to a "god" other than the one true God (i.e., worshiping an idol). They may not use those exact words, but whatever words they choose will likely convey that idea. And since they would never think of literally bowing down to an idol, they are convinced that they are not committing idolatry and that they are in no danger of ever doing so.

While in a general sense this explanation of idolatry may be accurate, the Holy Spirit reveals that idolatry has another dimension that few people probably think much about; and it is within that dimension that most contemporary Christians are vulnerable to committing idolatry. The Spirit reveals this other dimension of idolatry in Paul's letters to the Ephesians and Colossians. To the Ephesians he writes, "For this you know with certainty, that no immoral or impure person or *covetous man, who is an idolater*, has an inheritance in the kingdom of Christ and God" (Ephesians 5:5) (emphasis added). To the Colossians he writes, "Therefore consider the members of your earthly body as dead to immorality, impurity, passion, evil desire, and *greed, which amounts to idolatry*" (Colossians 3:5) (emphasis added).

What exactly does Paul mean when he says that greed is idolatry? Greed is an excessive and insatiable desire to have more. It may be more money, more prestige, more power, or more of just about anything. This insatiable and excessive desire for more prompts people to base virtually every day-to-day decision on getting what they desire rather than on doing what God desires. Because they make themselves "priority one," they are, in essence, worshiping themselves rather than God, and as John MacArthur says, "That is idolatry."[5]

So, this other dimension of idolatry that the Spirit is calling people's attention to seems clearly to be self-worship. It should also be noted that, unlike the pagan literally bowing down to an idol, a person can be "worshiping" himself and not even be conscious of it. There are no doubt many professing Christians who unknowingly offer God unacceptable worship on a regular basis because they have unconsciously placed themselves and their interests at the center of their attention and devotion. Knowing this danger, would-be worshipers must constantly examine their lives and hearts to ensure that they are basing their behavior and decisions on what God desires rather than on what they desire.

To summarize, God is not interested in the worship of a person who bows before an idol and calls it "Lord" and "Master." But perhaps more relevant to twenty-first century Christians in the west, God is not interested in the worship of a person who places himself at the center of his attention and devotion. Both practices constitute idolatry, and both render one's worship unacceptable.

Worthy and Properly Ordered Motives

A second principle of acceptable worship is that God must be worshiped for the right reasons. Some people may be under the impression that as long as they exclusively worship the one true God, it really does not matter why they worship Him. This impression, however, simply is not true.

The Scriptures identify at least one motive for worshiping which actually corrupts true worship and renders it unacceptable. What is that motive? It is worshiping in order to achieve an unworthy personal goal or receive unworthy personal rewards. When people use the occasion of worship primarily to achieve unworthy personal goals rather than to give praise and honor to God, God is simply not interested in their worship. They may achieve their desired goal, but they will *not* receive the approval of God. Jesus clearly implied this in His "Sermon of the Mount":

> And when you pray, you are not to be as the hypocrites; for they love to stand and pray in the synagogues and on the street corners, in order to be seen by men. Truly I say to you, they have their reward in full. But when you pray, go into your inner room, and when you have shut your door, pray to your Father

who is in secret, and your Father who sees in secret will repay you (Matthew 6:5-6).

In addition to having worthy motives when worshiping, worshipers must also properly prioritize their motives for worshiping. Since true worship is God-centered, no worship can be true when man replaces God as the central focus. And since true worship is God-serving, no worship can be true when people use the occasion primarily to serve themselves rather than God—even when the personal goals they seek are worthy.

Those who would aspire to be true worshipers frequently need to be reminded that worship must never be viewed primarily as means through which they can achieve personal goals or get some sort of personal reward. They must be taught that to view worship primarily as a self-serving, self-centered event corrupts worship by perverting its true meaning and purpose.

A Humble, Penitent Heart

A third principle of acceptable worship is that would-be worshipers must possess a heart that is characterized by humility and penitence. God is not interested in the worship of those whose hearts are full of arrogance and self-righteousness any more than He is interested in the worship of those who have placed themselves and their own interests at the center of worship.

The fact that God finds human arrogance and self-righteousness offensive is clearly taught throughout Scripture. For instance, the Psalmist says, "The Lord is near to the brokenhearted, and saves those who are crushed in spirit (Psalm 34:18). Similarly, Isaiah announces, "For thus says the high and exalted One who lives forever, whose name is Holy, 'I dwell on a high and holy place, and also with the contrite and lowly of spirit'" (Isaiah 57:15). Isaiah also says, "Thus says the Lord... 'to this one I will look, to him who is humble and contrite of spirit, and who trembles at My word' (Isaiah 66:2)."

When Christ preached His "Sermon on the Mount," the first thing He told His audience was that God favors those who have humble and penitent hearts. He said, "Blessed are the poor in spirit, for theirs is the kingdom of heaven," and "Blessed are those who mourn, for they shall be comforted" (Matthew 5:3-4). By these two statements Jesus simply means that any person who recognizes that he is destitute and spiritually impoverished apart from God, and mourns that condition, is truly fortunate.

The fact that a humble and penitent heart is essential to give value to one's worship is also clearly taught in Scripture. For instance, the Psalmist, presumably David, says, "For Thou dost not delight in sacrifice, otherwise I would give it; Thou art not pleased with burnt offering. The sacrifices of God are a broken spirit; a broken and contrite heart, O God, Thou wilt not despise" (Psalm 51:16-17).

Does this mean that God really does not care about one's expressions of worship? Of course not. It simply means that unless a person's expressions of praise are accompanied by a humble and penitent heart, God is not interested in it—it is nothing more than empty, mechanical ritual. Another way of expressing what the Psalmist is saying is that a person's disposition of mind gives value to his or her expressions of worship. A disposition of humility and penitence gives great value to them, while a disposition of arrogance and self-righteousness renders them worthless.

Perhaps nothing more clearly teaches that an arrogant and self-righteous heart renders one's worship unacceptable than the parable of the Pharisee and tax collector who went up to the temple to pray (i.e., worship). This parable, found in Luke 18:9-14, reads as follows:

> And He also told this parable to certain ones who trusted in themselves that they were righteous, and viewed others with contempt: Two men went up into the temple to pray, one a Pharisee, and the other a tax-gatherer. The Pharisee stood and was praying thus to himself, 'God, I thank Thee that I am not like

other people: swindlers, unjust, adulterers, or even like this tax-gatherer. I fast twice a week; I pay tithes of all that I get.' But the tax-gatherer, standing some distance away, was even unwilling to lift up his eyes to heaven, but was beating his breast, saying, 'God, be merciful to me, the sinner!' I tell you, this man went down to his house justified rather than the other; for everyone who exalts himself shall be humbled, but he who humbles himself shall be exalted.

Would-be worshipers must frequently be reminded to check their hearts for traces of arrogance and self-righteousness lest they stand before God in judgment only to find that their worship has been unacceptable because of these things. They must be told again and again that if their hearts are not characterized by humility and penitence as they approach God in worship, then God is not interested in their worship—no matter how carefully and closely they may follow the Biblically prescribed forms or expressions of worship.

A Godly Character of Life

A fourth fundamental principle, or essential ingredient, of acceptable worship is a godly character of life. In other words, those who would worship God acceptably must strive to live a life that reflects God's moral and ethical character. Just as God is not interested in the worship of one who places himself at the center of worship, and just as He is not interested in one's worship if it is accompanied by a haughty, proud spirit, so God also is not interested in one's worship if it is accompanied by a life of moral rebellion and ethical indifference.

The fact that God is not interested in a person's worship if his life is knowingly and persistently lived in moral rebellion is a common theme of Scripture. For instance, the writer of Proverbs proclaims, "To do righteousness and justice is desired by the Lord rather than sacrifice" (Proverbs 21:3). Similar to the idea expressed in Psalm 51:16-17, this proverb is simply saying that unless a person is striving to be morally and ethically excellent, God is not interested in what he is offering. Like worship which is offered by a proud, self-righteous person, worship which is offered by a moral rebel amounts to nothing more than empty, meaningless ritual.

During the eighth century B.C. Israel apparently thought it could make whatever moral and ethical choices it wanted and still worship God acceptably. Israel was wrong! Through Amos, God said to them,

> I hate, I reject your festivals, nor do I delight in your solemn assemblies. Even though you offer up to Me burnt offerings and your grain offerings, I will not accept them; and I will not even look at the peace offerings of your fatlings. Take away from Me the noise of your songs; I will not even listen to the sound of your harps. But let justice roll down like waters and righteousness like an ever-flowing stream (Amos 5:21-24).

Perhaps nowhere is there a more vivid portrayal of God's rejection of worship offered by immoral and unethical people than in Isaiah 1:11-17. Here Isaiah says to Judah,

> Hear the word of the Lord . . . 'What are your multiplied sacrifices to Me?' says the Lord. 'I have had enough of burnt offerings of rams, and the fat of fed cattle. And I take no pleasure in the blood of bulls, lambs, or goats. When you come to appear before Me, who requires of you this trampling of My courts? Bring your worthless offerings no longer, incense is an abomination to Me. New moon and sabbath, the calling of assemblies—I cannot endure iniquity and the solemn assembly. I hate your new moon festivals and your appointed feasts, they have become a burden to Me. I am weary of bearing them. So when you spread out your hands in prayer, I will hide My eyes from you, yes, even though you multiply prayers, I

will not listen. Your hands are covered with blood. Wash yourselves, make yourselves clean; remove the evil of your deeds from My sight. Cease to do evil, learn to do good; seek justice, reprove the ruthless; defend the orphan, plead for the widow.'

What exactly is this text saying? While the people of Judah were going through the outward, physical motions of worship, their lives were characterized by gross immorality. They would worship God one day and on the next be willing participants in moral and ethical atrocities. As a result, their worship was nothing more than a formal, empty show; it was a hypocritical sham, and God had no interest in it. To say it another way, because of their persistent immoral conduct and unethical behavior, God found their worship nauseating and unacceptable. The solution to this problem, Isaiah then tells them, is to repent of evil works and start living in harmony with God's moral and ethical character.

Unfortunately, several years later the people of Judah were still going through the outward motions of worship, but they still had not brought their lives into harmony with God's moral and ethical will. At this point God describes them as follows: "For from the least of them even to the greatest of them, everyone is greedy for gain, and from the prophet even to the priest everyone deals falsely" (Jeremiah 6:13). Consequently, God still refused to accept their worship. To Him it was still a hypocritical, offensive sham. He said to them, "For what purpose does frankincense come to Me from Sheba, and the sweet cane from a distant land? Your burnt offerings are not acceptable, and your sacrifices are not pleasing to Me" (Jeremiah 6:20).

The principle that acceptable worship demands a godly character also seems to be taught clearly in the New Testament when Peter says, "You husbands likewise, live with your wives in an understanding way, as with a weaker vessel, since she is a woman; and grant her honor as a fellow heir of the grace of life, so that your prayers may not be hindered" (1 Peter 3:7). The Holy Spirit's message in this passage seems clear and simple—if a man does not treat his wife with the dignity, respect, compassion, kindness, and gentleness that she deserves, then God simply is not interested in his prayers (i.e., his worship).

Another New Testament passage which seems to have relevance to this point, despite the fact that worship is not specifically mentioned in it, is Luke 10:29-37. In this passage Jesus relates the parable of the "good Samaritan." As every Bible student knows, in this parable there were two men who, as they traveled, came upon, and yet ignored, another man who had been beaten and left for dead by a band of outlaws. As every Bible student also knows, these two men were part of the "religious establishment"—one was a priest, the other a Levite. In other words, they were among the most devout worshipers of their day.

Although the primary aim of this parable is to teach people who their "neighbors" are, as well as teach them how they should behave toward them, it also clearly seems to imply that if a person's behavior does not reflect the moral and ethical character of God, then God is *not* pleased with him—even if he is a regular and devoted worshiper of God.

Responsive to God's Will

A fifth ingredient of acceptable worship is that would-be worshipers must be responsive to the will of God. That is, they must desire to know God's will and do it in every circumstance of life. A perfect example of such a person was Ezra. The Scriptures say, "For Ezra set his heart to study the law of the Lord, and to practice it, and to teach His statutes and ordinances in Israel" (Ezra 7:10).

The writer of the 119th Psalm also embodied what it means to be responsive to the will of God. Although his responsiveness to the will of God is reflected in virtually every verse of the chapter, consider what he writes in the ninth through the sixteenth verses:

How can a young man keep his way pure? By keeping it according to Thy word. With all my heart I have sought Thee; do not let me wander from Thy commandments. Thy word I have treasured in my heart, that I may not sin against Thee. Blessed art Thou, O Lord; teach me Thy statutes. With my lips I have told of all the ordinances of Thy mouth. I have rejoiced in the way of Thy testimonies, as much as in all riches. I will meditate on Thy precepts, and regard Thy ways. I shall delight in Thy statutes; I shall not forget Thy word.

His thoughts in verses thirty-three through forty also magnificently display a responsiveness to the will of God. Here he writes,

Teach me, O Lord, the way of Thy statutes, and I shall observe it to the end. Give me understanding, that I may observe Thy law, and keep it with all my heart. Make me walk in the path of Thy commandments, for I delight in it. Incline my heart to Thy testimonies, and not to dishonest gain. Turn away my eyes from looking at vanity, and revive me in Thy ways. Establish Thy word to Thy servant, as that which produces reverence for Thee. Turn away my reproach which I dread, for Thine ordinances are good. Behold, I long for Thy precepts; revive me through Thy righteousness.

The fact that God is not interested in the worship of those who are generally indifferent toward knowing and doing His will could not be made more clear than it is in Proverbs 28:9. Here the Holy Spirit warns, "He who turns away his ear from listening to the law, even his prayer is an abomination." It seems quite clear that the idea being expressed here is that God will not respond to those who are not responsive to His will. In other words, worship will have real value only when the one offering it seeks to know and do the will of God above all else.

Of course, it should be noted that this does not mean that a person must have an exhaustive, perfect knowledge of the will of God and never make a mistake—neither attribute is possible. It simply means that true worshipers must be committed to growing in their knowledge of God's will and equally committed to obeying the commands of God in all things.

Another place where Scripture seems clearly to teach that God is not interested in people's worship if they are not responsive to His will is in Matthew 15:1-10. On this occasion a group of Pharisees and scribes confronted Jesus with the accusation that His disciples were transgressing the tradition of the elders. In part, Jesus' response to them was, ". . . you invalidate the word of God for the sake of your tradition. You hypocrites, rightly did Isaiah prophesy of you, saying, 'This people honors Me with their lips, but their heart is far away from Me. But in vain do they worship Me, teaching as doctrines the precepts of men'" (v. 9).

Like many during Isaiah's day, these Pharisees and scribes made a show of devotion to God, but their true devotion was to a faith system which was clearly a product of men. In other words, they had a self-styled faith system that took precedence over God's will. They were more interested in knowing, keeping, and promoting the will of certain men than in knowing, keeping, and promoting the will of God. Because they were more responsive to a faith system which had been shaped and styled by men than to the one shaped and styled by God, Jesus told them that their worship to God was worthless.

Divinely Prescribed Expressions

Recalling that worship must involve an expression of praise, I am convinced that worshipers must offer praise to God *only* through actions and expressions which He has expressly prescribed or commanded. Although this principle is not explicitly *stated* in Scripture, at least two things in Scripture seem clearly to imply it.

First, God spent a great deal of time with Moses laying out in exacting detail the outward actions, rites, and ceremonies through which Israel was to approach and worship Him (e.g., Leviticus 1-3; 2 Chronicles 29:25). Why would He have done this if the decision in these matters rested with Israel? The fact that God clearly gave them specific guidance in the matter of outward forms and expressions of worship would seem to argue that He never intended for them to decide these matters for themselves.

Second, Leviticus 10:1 records that as Nadab and Abihu, the two sons of Aaron the high priest, were to lead the people in worship, they took their firepans, put fire in them, placed incense on them, and offered it to the Lord. The text then records that their offering was something which "He [God] had not commanded them." Consequently, verse two says, "And fire came out from the presence of the Lord and consumed them, and they died before the Lord." This event clearly shows that God expected Nadab and Abihu to offer only those things which He had expressly commanded.

Based on these examples, some may be willing to acknowledge that Old Testament saints were limited only to forms and expressions of worship which God expressly commanded, yet continue to question whether New Testament saints are similarly limited.

In response to their questioning the validity of this principle for the "church age," I would first observe that there is nothing in the New Testament which suggests that this principle passed away with the Old Testament faith system. In other words, there is neither a clear statement nor even a vague implication in the New Testament which suggests that, unlike Old Testament saints, Christians have the liberty to decide for themselves how they will express their praise and devotion to God. Is it not reasonable to think that if God intended to leave this principle in the Old Testament—that is, not bring it into the "church age"—He would have somehow communicated this intent?

I would also observe that, just as God issued specific instructions when He revealed His will to Israel, in the New

Testament God is detailed and exact: He does not simply give His people generic commands to worship. Instead, He gives them specific direction regarding, among other things, forms and expressions of worship.

For instance, in Colossians 3:16 and Ephesians 5:19, God commands Christians to sing praises to Him. In passages such as Ephesians 6:18, Philippians 4:6, Colossians 4:2, and 1 Thessalonians 5:17, He commands them to pray. In 1 Corinthians 11:23ff, He commands them to proclaim their faith in the past, present, and future work of Christ by eating unleavened bread and drinking fruit of the vine. Why does God do this if He intended for believers to choose their own forms and expressions of worship? The fact that God has given His church specific guidance in these matters would seem to argue that they are not at liberty to decide these things for themselves.

Why did God—both in the Old Testament and the New—give His people specific guidance regarding forms and expressions of worship? Why did He not merely give them a generic command to worship and stop there, thus leaving the matter of choosing forms and expressions of worship to their discretion? Unfortunately, He never reveals why—either in the Old Testament or the New. Perhaps, however, it would not be too inappropriate to speculate about the answer.

I would suggest that if man were given the liberty to choose the forms and expressions through which he would worship God, he would inevitably choose forms and expressions which would satisfy his own personal tastes and interests. This would only encourage man to place himself, rather than God, at the center of the worship experience. However, if God dictates the forms and expressions through which man must worship, man is constantly reminded that God is the center the worship, that God is Lord and Master, and that man is merely God's obedient servant. Even if this is not the right answer, it is an idea that seems worthy of some consideration.

Before concluding this chapter, it is important to discuss briefly the application of this principle. How should one apply the principle that true worshipers must restrict their expressions of worship only to those expressions which have been prescribed or commanded by God? In a word, I believe the principle must be applied *strictly*.

What exactly do I mean by the term "strictly"? Perhaps an illustration will best explain it. I have no choice but to reject the common practice of praising God with musical instruments since there is no prescription or command for that form or expression of praise in the entire New Testament. There are commands to sing praises to God (Ephesians 5:19; Colossians 3:16), as well as examples of Christians praising Him in song (Acts 16:25; 1 Corinthians 14:15,26), but there is not a single command to praise Him with musical instruments, nor a single example of Christians praising Him in that manner. As LaGard Smith says,

> In contrast to the many Old Testament passages referring to musical instruments in temple worship, in the New Testament text not one sound of a musical instrument is heard—not a trumpet, not a harp, not the quietest jingle of a tambourine! Singing, yes. Musical instruments, no. Relative to musical instruments, there is only an ominous haunting silence.[6]

Even proponents of praising God with musical instruments must acknowledge that there is no prescription or support for the practice in the New Testament. For instance, in a class on "Church Music" which I sat in on at Grace Theological Seminary, the professor distributed and discussed an outline entitled "Music in the Church." The first part of his outline reads as follows:

1a. Why?
1b. Scriptural command
    Vocal - Psalm 96:1, 100:1,2; Eph. 5:19; Col. 3:16
    Instrumental - Psalm 150:3-5[7]

Note that this professor distinguished between "vocal" and "instrumental" music. Despite the fact that vocal and instrumental music are usually combined in contemporary western culture, they *are* different musical forms. His distinction, therefore, is appropriate. Also, note that the only command he cites for "Instrumental" music is from the Old Testament. On this point he offered an unsolicited comment that was brief but interesting. He said, "It is true that there is no New Testament authority for instrumental music, but there is in the Old Testament and I believe it is the same."[8] He then said that the question of whether or not the church should use instrumental music in worship used to be a "big deal," but it is not any longer; and with that comment he proceeded to discuss other topics.

Although my position on the matter of praising God with musical instruments is currently a minority view among contemporary "Christians" in the western world, it should be noted that it is the view that has been held by the vast majority of Christians for over twenty centuries. In fact, although virtually every Protestant denomination today officially sanctions the practice of praising God with musical instruments, it is interesting to note that their founders and leaders almost uniformly rejected the practice.

Perhaps the most glaring confirmation of the fact that the majority of Christians have historically rejected worshiping or praising God with musical instruments is found in the words *a capella*. *Cappella* is Latin for *chapel* or *church*. Taken literally, the Italian *a cappella* means "in chapel style," or "in the style of the church." As LaGard Smith notes,

From the first century onward, vocal music was so distinctive from the instrumental music used in both pagan worship and private entertainment that it was uniquely known as music of the church—that is, *a cappella*! So when we say that we sing *a cappella*, we are affirming what millions of believers over centuries have affirmed—that the music of the church is distinctively vocal![9]

I realize, of course, that not everyone would agree with this application of the principle. For instance, consider what John MacArthur has to say about acceptable and unacceptable worship: "God will not accept the worship of a false god, nor will He accept the worship of the true God if offered in the wrong way. Why? Because the worship of the true God is very specifically established in Scripture, along with the proper mode and manner."[10]

Then, after discussing the account of Nadab and Abihu in Leviticus 10:1-2, MacArthur contends, "God will not accept self-styled, self-invented modes of worship. We are not to worship God on our own terms; we are to worship Him according to the terms prescribed in Scripture."[11] Still further in his discussion he says, "So, what I'm trying to show you is that there is a category of unacceptable worship. One cannot worship false gods or the true God in a wrong form or in a self-styled manner. It must be according to the prescription of Scripture."[12]

These statements clearly show that MacArthur embraces the principle that true worshipers must restrict their modes or expressions of worship only to those which have been expressly prescribed or commanded by God. At the same time, however, he endorses worshiping God with musical instruments—a form of praise for which, as just observed, there is absolutely no New Testament prescription.

His endorsement of this form of praise is evident from a statement he makes in his book *Ashamed of the Gospel*. After promoting much of what the famous nineteenth century Baptist evangelist Charles Spurgeon had to say in regard to worship, MacArthur notes in a section entitled "Is All Innovation Wrong?" that "Spurgeon himself would not appreciate our organ."[13] His point was that although he believes many contemporary trends in public worship need to be challenged, he does not believe that all innovation in worship is wrong—even innovations which someone of Spurgeon's stature may object to—like praising God with musical instruments.

For those like MacArthur who seem to embrace the "true-worship-requires-divinely-prescribed-expressions" principle, but seem to reject my strict application of it, I would suggest that the nature of the principle prohibits any application other than a strict one. After all, to argue that true worshipers must restrict their modes or expressions of worship only to those which have been specifically prescribed by God, and yet at the same time argue that it is acceptable to worship God through some forms and expressions which He has *not* prescribed makes no logical sense. It is a contradictory position. If the principle is going to be embraced, its logical end must also be embraced.

For those still reluctant to accept the validity of this principle, or for those still reluctant to accept a strict application of it, I would suggest that there is another reason to restrict one's expressions of worship only to those which have been specifically prescribed by God. What is that reason? When a worshiper offers adoration and praise to God only through expressions which He has clearly commanded, that worshiper can be sure that God will be pleased rather than offended with his offering. This assumes, of course, that his motives for worshiping are worthy and properly prioritized and that his expressions of worship are accompanied by a humble and penitent heart, a godly character of life, a heart that is devoted solely to God, and a submissive will. Although the experience of Nadab and Abihu (Leviticus 10:1-2) is more than thirty-five centuries old, it still convinces me that I do not wish to risk the possibility of offending God by offering Him something which He has not commanded.

Some may think that having a guarantee that God will be pleased is not really a sufficient reason to limit modes or expressions of worship only to those which are found in the

New Testament. I, however, cannot think of a better reason to do so. The ultimate aspiration of every Christian should be to please God. Paul prayed that the Colossians would "walk in a manner worthy of the Lord, to please Him in all respects" (Colossians 1:10). He told the Thessalonians that they received from him instructions "as to how you ought to walk and please God . . . " (1 Thessalonians 4:1). And John wrote, ". . . whatever we ask we receive from Him, because we keep His commandments and do the things that are pleasing in His sight" (1 John 3:22).

With these admonitions in mind, why would any would-be disciple reject a course which he *knows* will please God for a course which cannot make that guarantee? As Jack Lewis observes, "One can only know a thing is pleasing to God—no matter how beautiful and appealing it may be in his own eyes—when God has said that it is pleasing."[14]

To me, this matter seems very analogous to a traveler who comes to a fork in the road as he is trying to reach a particular destination. Unfortunately, there are no signs at the fork to point him in the right direction. Not knowing, therefore, which way he should go, he has no choice but to stop and consult a map. As he does so, much to his surprise, he sees that only one of the two roads which comprise the fork is on the map. Fortunately, however, he sees that this road will definitely lead him to his destination.

After examining the map, how many travelers would forgo the road they know leads to their destination, and instead opt for the other—although they have no objective proof that it will lead them where they want to go? I am confident that the answer would be "very few." Few are willing to risk getting lost and failing to reach their destination. Simply put, when traveling, most people like guarantees (i.e., "sure things").

The consequences of not pleasing God are certainly more dire than getting lost on the way to a geographic destination. Knowing the seriousness of the matter, surely no one would want to risk those consequences if they can possibly be avoided—and they can. By restricting one's expressions of adoration and praise only to those expressions which are specifically commanded by God, worshipers will be traveling a road for which there is clear and objective proof that it leads to their desired destination—pleasing God.

Questions to Guide Study

1. What is the ultimate standard by which all worship must be measured? What are some implications of this answer?

2. Why does God refuse to share reverence with anyone or anything?

3. Do you think contemporary Christians in the west are very susceptible to committing idolatry? Explain.

4. What must worship never be viewed as? Why?

5. What is the relationship between a person's heart (i.e., disposition of mind) and his or her worship? Support your answer with Biblical data.

6. What is the relationship between a person's character of life and his or her worship? Support your answer with Biblical data.

7. What does it mean to be responsive to God's will? Give a Biblical example of someone who was clearly responsive to God's will.

8. What Biblical evidence suggests that a person's outward forms and expressions of worship must be divinely prescribed?

9. Discuss the application of the principle stated in question #8.

10. Pragmatically speaking, why is it best to restrict one's forms and expressions of worship only to those which God has specifically prescribed?

Endnotes

[1] Donald Guthrie, *The Pastoral Epistles*, vol. 14 in the Tyndale New Testament Commentary series (Grand Rapids: Eerdmans, 1990), 70-71.

[2] Ibid, 71.

[3] In this instance the word *proskeneo* may reflect a very respectful greeting rather than worship. Peter's response to it, however, shows that even if this is the case, he thought it was too much reverence to give a man.

[4] Jack Cottrell, *What the Bible Says About God the Creator* (Joplin, MO: College Press, 1983), 161.

[5] John MacArthur, Jr., *Colossians and Philemon*, The MacArthur New Testament Commentary series (Chicago: Moody Press, 1992), 139.

[6] LaGard Smith, *The Cultural Church* (Nashville, TN: 20th Century Christian, 1992), 199.

[7] The professor's original outline is in my possession.

[8] This statement shows a failure to recognize the difference between the nature of the Old and New Covenants. Although New Testament saints can learn many truths about God, man, sin, and salvation from a careful and thorough study of the Old Testament (Romans 15:4), God never intended for its specific tenets to be the permanent standard for His people's life and worship. It ceased to be a binding law for God's people after Messiah came and finished His work at Calvary (Hebrews 9:15; 10:9; Colossians 2:13-14). Therefore, although the basic *principles* of acceptable worship did not change when the Old Covenant was replaced by the New, it is *not* appropriate for a Christian to "reach back" into the Old Testament and shape the *specific elements* of his worship according to the *specific elements and tenets* of the temple worship system. Christians must shape their worship solely according to the inspired, apostolic writings of the Christian age (i.e., the New Testament). For those who believe God's commands for specific elements and tenets of worship under the Old Testament system are still binding and valid on worshipers in the church age, I would like to ask why their services do not perfectly parallel tabernacle or temple worship?

[9] LaGard Smith, *The Cultural Church* (Nashville, TN: 20th Century Christian, 1992), 201.

[10]John MacArthur, Jr., *True Worship* in John MacArthur's Bible Study series (Chicago: Moody Press, 1982), 19.

[11]Ibid., 21.

[12]Ibid., 23.

[13]John MacArthur, Jr., *Ashamed of the Gospel: When the Church Becomes Like the World* (Wheaton, IL: Crossway Books, 1993), xviii.

[14]Jack Lewis, "Reformation Thought," *Gospel Advocate* vol. 138, no. 1 (January 1996): 19. In this article Lewis examines the principle of silence in the Scripture and its effects on Reformation thought.

Chapter 12
Blessed By Worship

The fact that worship must not be viewed primarily as an occasion to get personal rewards does not mean that worship does not have its personal rewards. As noted earlier, God has so designed worship that true worshipers will receive many personal blessings as they honor and glorify Him in the sphere of worship. In this chapter I want to discuss what I believe to be some of those blessings.

Through Worship a Person's Knowledge and Understanding of God Significantly Increase

One blessing of worship is that through it a person's knowledge and understanding of God significantly increase. When a person reads and meditates on Scripture, listens to strong, Biblical preaching and teaching, and sings hymns that celebrate God's work, nature, and attributes, God as creator, ruler, and redeemer comes into sharper focus. In other words, through a recital of God's past, present, and future work in human history, His power, holiness, justice, mercy, graciousness, goodness, and other attributes are magnified and meditated upon. As a result, the true worshiper comes to know and understand God as He really is—at least to the extent that a finite person can know and understand the infinite God.

There are many reasons to consider this intensified apprehension of God to be among the most valuable and coveted blessings that a person could ever receive (cf. Jeremiah 9:23-24). What are they? For one thing, knowing and understanding God as He truly is brings great comfort. For instance, what could be more comforting for a person than to know and appreciate the fact that God is personally concerned about him (Matthew 6:25-34), or that God desires to save, rather than punish him (1 Timothy 2:4; 2 Peter 3:9), or that God has provided him with everything necessary to reach his fullest spiritual potential (Colossians 2:10; 2 Timothy 3:16-17)? And what could be more comforting than to know and appreciate the fact that God is always willing to forgive and extend mercy (1 John 1:9; Matthew 18:21-35), or that He will never allow Satan to tempt a person beyond what he can endure (1 Corinthians 10:13), or that He is in complete control of all things, and that His purposes can never be thwarted by anyone or anything (Daniel 4:34-35)?

Also, knowing and understanding God inspires trust and confidence in Him. God calls people to trust Him for their salvation (Jeremiah 17:5-8; John 3:16); and when one comes to know God through His work in human history, any uncertainty about His desire or ability to really save will vanish. When one knows and understands God as He truly is, he will never question whether God *can* really save him or *will* really save him. He knows that God can do whatever He wills (Daniel 4:35; Psalm 115:3; 135:6) and that He never breaks a promise (2 Timothy 2:13; Titus 1:2; Hebrews 6:18).

Another blessing of knowing and understanding God is that expanded awareness cultivates respect and reverence for Him. Reverence for God is vital if one expects to have a healthy relationship with God. The Scriptures clearly teach that those who worship and serve Him must do so with reverence and awe (Psalm 2:11; Hebrews 12:28). With this admonition in mind, there is really only one way to cultivate such an attitude in would-be disciples—help them know, understand, and appreciate God as He truly is. When one comes to know God as He truly is, reverence and awe will naturally result. In other words, to know God is to revere God. In fact, reverence for God is so dependent on a knowledge and understanding of Him that it is safe to say that a person who does not have a deep respect and reverence for God does not know and understand Him. That person may know something *about* God, but a superficial acquaintance does not mean he truly knows and understands Him.

Still another blessing of knowing and understanding God is that it cultivates in the disciple a desire to worship Him. Unlike David, who said, "I was glad when they said to me, 'Let us go to the house of the Lord'" (Psalm 122:1), many professing Christians view worship as a burden to bear or as a "square to fill" on the road to eternal life. Why is such a negative view of worship so prevalent? There can be little doubt that it is largely because there is a dearth of knowledge and understanding of God both within the church and throughout the wider "Christian" community.

Several years ago in *The Witness*, Curtis Dickinson asked, "What's Happened to God?" He lamented the fact that "even among people who regularly attend church there is little understanding of God."[1] Years later I have the same concern. Dickinson continued:

> . . . They are engaged in 'church activities,' given pep talks, how-to-do-it lectures and conversion sermons; they are encouraged to pray to God, to be godly, and to win others to God; they are to give to God, serve God, and desire to see Him and spend eternity with Him; but seldom if ever are they taught anything about Him, His nature and His attributes. It is no wonder that many churches have to give prizes to get people to ride their buses to the church house.[2]

Just as there is only one way to cultivate within a person an attitude of reverence and awe, there is really only one way to cultivate within a person a desire to worship God—

help him know and understand God as He truly is. If churches will regularly and frequently teach about God— His work, His nature, and His attributes—it is unlikely that they will have to rely so heavily on fear motivation, or have to appeal so strongly to Christian duty, to get people to assemble for worship. If people really knew, understood, and appreciated God, the question, "Do I have to go to church?" would never be heard. When a person really knows and understands God, he will, like David, actually desire and anticipate occasions to worship Him.

A fifth blessing of knowing and understanding God is that it helps one understand and appreciate the seriousness of sin. Those who know and understand God as He truly is know that He is infinitely holy (Isaiah. 6:3; Revelation 4:8). In part this means that God is morally perfect, or as Jack Cottrell says, "absolute ethical perfection and purity, that he is unconditionally upright in his essence and in his actions. He is the ultimate standard of rectitude and integrity."[3] It also means that God has an absolute hatred of and aversion to sin (Romans 1:18; Colossians 3:6; Ephesians 5:3-6).

The fact that God is so totally separate from sin in His nature, His will, and His action means that He can never look with favor on those who are marred by sin; that is, He can never allow those who have the guilt of sin upon them to live in His presence (Isaiah 59:2; Hebrews 1:13). How does such an awareness of the nature of sin bless people? For one thing, it challenges them not to be indifferent toward sin or take it lightly. Also, it provokes them constantly to examine their lives for the presence of sin—both "glaring" and "subtle" sin; and when they do sin, it urges them to move swiftly to seek forgiveness. Finally, despite knowing that they will still occasionally sin, it inspires them to guard their lives closely against the intrusion of sin.

Sixth and finally, knowing and understanding God will inspire people to pursue holiness. God's desire for His people is that they be holy as He is holy (Romans 12:1; 2 Corinthians 7:1; Ephesians 1:4; 5:27; Colossians 1:22; 1 Thessalonians 4:3; 1 Peter 1:15-16). When a person, through worship, "sees" and meditates on the holy and blameless character of God, especially as seen through the life and work of Jesus Christ (John 10:30; 14:9-10; Colossians 1:15), he is often aroused and motivated to imitate God's moral character. It works in much the same way that an aspiring musician or athlete is motivated to strive toward excellence by watching the performance of a world-class musician or athlete.

Through Worship a Person Recognizes His Sinfulness and Unworthiness to Be in God's Presence

Another blessing of worship is that in an encounter with the infinitely holy God a person sees himself in all his sin and recognizes that he is unworthy to be in God's presence. For example, when Peter was confronted with a miracle which showed Jesus to be Messiah, he fell on his face and cried, "Depart from me, for I am a sinful man, O Lord" (Luke 5:8). Similarly, when Isaiah witnessed the glory and majesty of God he cried, "Woe is me, for I am ruined! Because I am a man of unclean lips, and I live among a people of unclean lips; for my eyes have seen the King, the Lord of hosts" (Isaiah 6:5).

To some, especially to those of the world, such a realization about oneself may not sound like a blessing; but the value of recognizing one's own sinfulness and unworthiness to be in God's presence is beyond measure. Why? For one thing, those who recognize and appreciate their sinfulness will recognize and appreciate their need for forgiveness; and those who recognize and appreciate their need for forgiveness are likely aggressively to seek and ultimately to find it in Christ Jesus. On the other hand, those who do not recognize and appreciate their own personal sinfulness will never recognize their need for forgiveness; and those who never recognize their need for forgiveness will never seek or obtain it.

Also, a recognition and appreciation of one's sinfulness and unworthiness to be in God's presence promotes a spirit of humility that must characterize those who seek to follow

Christ. Those who fail to recognize and appreciate their sinfulness, however, can easily become proud and haughty, and they will never find favor with God as long as such an attitude persists. This principle is clearly taught by Christ in the parable of the Pharisee and the tax-collector who went to the temple to pray (Luke 18:9-14). Jesus said the Pharisee stood and thanked God that he was not like other sinners, including the tax-collector. He also boasted to God about his regular participation in spiritual activities such as fasting and paying tithes. The tax-collector, however, felt too unworthy to lift his eyes to heaven. Instead, he beat his breast and cried out, "God, be merciful to me, the sinner!" Jesus then said, "I tell you, this man [the tax-collector] went down to his house justified rather than the other; for everyone who exalts himself shall be humbled, but he who humbles himself shall be exalted" (v. 14).

The fact that a humble and broken spirit is important to God is also reflected in the first words that came out of Jesus' mouth as He preached His "Sermon on the Mount": "Blessed (i.e., fortunate) are the poor in spirit, for theirs is the kingdom of heaven" (Matthew 5:3). The Psalmist likewise expresses this fact when he says, "For though the Lord is exalted, yet He regards the lowly; but the haughty He knows from afar" (Psalm 138:6; cf. James 4:6).

Finally, when one recognizes and appreciates the fact that he is unworthy to be in God's presence, yet understands and appreciates the fact that God not only wants him to come into His presence (Hebrews 4:15-16), but that He has provided a way for him to do so (Hebrews 10:19-25), that person will likely be overwhelmed with deep gratitude. This deep gratitude in turn will often foster a strong desire to worship and serve God more faithfully.

Before moving on, it should be emphasized that merely recognizing one's sinfulness and unworthiness to be in God's presence will not necessarily prompt a person to seek forgiveness or to be humble or to worship and serve God more faithfully. In other words, these kinds of responses are not necessarily aroused by an intellectual awareness of being a sinner and of being unworthy, therefore, to be in God's presence.

As stated throughout this section, it also takes an intellectual and emotional *appreciation* of these things. Although this section began with the assertion, "through worship a person recognizes his sinfulness and unworthiness to be in God's presence," I would also suggest that worship moves a person from the mere intellectual recognition of these things to an emotional appreciation of them as nothing else can.

Through Worship a Person Is Reminded That He Has Great Intrinsic Value and That God Is Genuinely Interested in Him

Another blessing of worship is that through it a person will inevitably be confronted with many facts which remind him that he has great intrinsic worth and that God is genuinely and passionately interested in his well-being (Matthew 6:25-26). For instance, as one worships he will inevitably be confronted with the fact that he has been created by God in the very image of God to rule and have dominion over every other living thing (Genesis 1:26-28). He will be confronted with the fact that when man sinned and could no longer live in God's presence, God cared so deeply that He initiated a plan that would allow man to return and once again experience fellowship with Him (Genesis 3:15; 12:3). He will be confronted with the fact that from the moment man fell, God's work in history has pointed to the single goal of saving man from his sins (Matthew 1:21). He will be confronted with the fact that Jesus voluntarily gave up equality with God for a time and endured death on a cross just to save him (Philippians 2:5-8; Galatians 2:20). And he will be confronted with the fact that one person is so important to God that there is more joy in heaven over one sinner who repents than over ninety-nine who need no repentance (Luke 15:7).

Like the two blessings of worship which have already been discussed, this blessing also has its own personal rewards. What are they? For one thing, the person who knows that he has great intrinsic value and that God is personally concerned about him will be filled with overwhelming joy. Of course this does not mean that he will never experience feelings of sadness. The life of every person is full of circumstances which at times will fill him with anger, sadness, pain, and grief. It is simply saying that within those who know that God is passionately concerned about them, there is at some level a sense of well-being and a feeling of gladness which will always be present regardless of the circumstances of life in which they find themselves.

Another blessing of knowing that God cares for each person and that each person has great intrinsic worth is that this knowledge brings great emotional comfort to a person. What could be more comforting to a person than the knowledge that in his most difficult and lonely times God is very much aware of his situation and needs (Matthew 6:8,32), that He cares deeply (1 Peter 5:7), and that He is working eventually to bring something good out of even the most adverse circumstances (Romans 8:28)?

A third blessing of being conscious of one's intrinsic worth, as well as being conscious of God's concern for each person, is that it tends to fill one with awe, wonder, and gratitude. When a person meditates on the fact that the infinite God not only made him (Jeremiah 1:5), but also loves him (Romans 8:37; Galatians 2:20), and longs to have a personal relationship with him (Matthew 11:28-30; Hosea 1-14), feelings of awe and gratitude are quite natural (cf. Galatians 2:20). And as was said before, such deep gratitude tends to foster within a person a strong desire to worship and serve God more faithfully.

Fourth, the person who knows and appreciates the fact that he has great intrinsic worth and that God personally cares for him will be inspired to excel spiritually. That is, the one who knows that God loves him (Romans 5:8), cares for him (1 Peter 5:7), "cheers" for him (1 Timothy 2:4; 2 Peter 3:9), and helps him in his spiritual fight (1 Corinthians 10:13; 1 Peter 1:5; Jude 24; Hebrews 1:14) is much more likely to bring all his effort and energy to bear upon his quest for eternal life than the person who thinks he is running alone, or at least running with very little help from God.

Fifth and finally, the person who is conscious of his great intrinsic worth and the fact that God personally cares for him will recognize that every other person is equally valuable to God, and he will subsequently treat each one in a manner which reflects his value and worth, as well as the fact that God is personally interested in everyone (Matthew 18:10). A person who is aware of his own intrinsic worth will see as much value in the poor as in the rich. He will see as much value in the homely as in the handsome. He will see as much value in the child whose mental development has been retarded as in the child prodigy. He will see as much value in the child in the womb as in the child outside the womb. He will see as much value in people of other races and ethnic origins as in people of his own race and ethnic origin. He will see as much value in the old and feeble as in the young and strong. He will see as much value in the sick and dying as in the healthy. And, most significantly, his behavior toward all of these will reflect that conviction.

Through Worship a Christian Is Reminded of His Privileged Position in Christ

Still another blessing of worship is that through it a Christian is constantly reminded of his privileged position in Christ. That is, as a person praises God for His saving work through Christ (1 Peter 1:3-5; Romans 5:1-2, 8-11), listens to Scripture being read and expounded, and eats the Lord's Supper, he will regularly be made aware of all the privileges and blessings that are found in Christ; and when a knowledge of these things is coupled with an appreciation for them, a person will be impacted positively in several ways.

For one thing, he will be prompted to live a life that is characterized by worship and sacrificial service. When a person contemplates and appreciates the fact that in Christ he has been shown mercy, he will, like Paul, be overwhelmed with awe and frequently burst forth in praise (Romans 11:32-36). Also, when a person contemplates and appreciates this fact, he will respond with a life of sacrificial service. The person who truly appreciates the blessings that he has been given in Christ knows that a life of sacrificial service is one of the only responses congruous with God's bestowing of those blessings (Romans 12:1-2).

Also, an awareness and appreciation of the privileges that one has in Christ will bring a person great emotional comfort or peace of mind (Romans 14:7; 15:13; Phil. 4:7). What could bring more emotional tranquility to a person than a knowledge and appreciation of the fact that in Christ the sins that separated him from God are forgiven (Ephesians. 1:7), that he is in no danger of eternal condemnation (Romans 8:1), and that when Jesus comes again, he will be taken up to meet the Lord in the air and "thus . . . shall always be with the Lord" (1 Thessalonians 4:13-18)? And what could bring more peace of mind to a person than a knowledge and appreciation of the fact that in Christ he has God's approving love and that nothing or no one can separate him from that love (Romans 8:35-39).

Finally, an awareness and appreciation of the privileges and blessings that one has in Christ will fill a person with great joy (Romans 14:7; 15:13; Galatians 5:22). In other words, when one contemplates and appreciates the blessings of being in Christ which were just mentioned, along with the fact that in Christ he is an heir (Galatians 3:26-29) to an inheritance that is "imperishable and undefiled and will not fade away" (1 Peter 1:4), overwhelming joy is the natural result. Of course, it is important to remember that, as stated earlier, this does not mean that one will be immune to emotions such as sadness or that a person will incessantly be outwardly expressing delight. It simply means that within those who appreciate the significance of being in Christ, there is a deep-down sense of well-being and a gladness in their heart, which is always present and independent of any external circumstances.

Through Worship a Person Will Be Prompted to View Life From an Eternal Perspective

Another blessing of worship is that through it a person will inevitably be confronted with truths that will prompt him to view life from an eternal perspective. For one thing, he will often be confronted with the fact that death is his destiny (Psalm 49:10; Ecclesiastes 2:14; 3:19-20; 6:6; 9:2-2; Hebrews 9:27). Also, he will be confronted with the fact that after death he will stand before God and have his life judged (Matthew 16:27; Romans 2:16; 14:10-12; 2 Corinthians 5:9-10; Hebrews 9:27). And finally, he will be confronted with the fact that, based on his life, God will consign him to heaven or hell for all eternity (Matthew 25:31-46; John 5:28-29; Matthew 19:29; John 3:16,36; 5:24; 6:27,40,47,54; Romans 2:5-8).

The obvious benefit of viewing life through these truths is that it tends to inspire a person to live in such a way that when he stands before God he will hear the words, "Come, you who are blessed of My Father, inherit the kingdom prepared for you from the foundation of the world" (Matthew 25:34). In other words, it tends to inspire a person to pursue the things in life that matter most to God.

Those who appreciate the fact that they will stand before God in judgement will *not* be so concerned with how many degrees they have earned, or how far up the corporate ladder they have climbed, or how good their golf game is, or how much money they make, or how well traveled they are, or how big and beautiful their house is. The primary concerns of these people will include more eternally significant considerations: "Am I the kind of parent and spouse God wants me to be?" "Am I the kind of neighbor, citizen, and employee or employer God wants me to be?" "Have I responded to Christ's work at Calvary by obeying the gospel?", "Does my life reflect the moral and ethical character of God?" "Am I trying to do the will of God in all things—socially, morally, ethically, and religiously?" "Have I found a place within the body of Christ where my talents and abilities can best be utilized?" and "Am I using my talents and abilities to their fullest potential for Christ?"

At least one more benefit of viewing life from an eternal perspective is that it tends to inspire people to guard their lives against the intrusion of sin and to seek forgiveness when it does intrude. In other words, the person who knows and appreciates the fact that his eternal destiny will be determined, in part, by his words (Matthew 12:36) and deeds (Romans 2:5-6) will closely guard these things against Satan's corrupting influence. And when this person sins—and he will (1 John 1:8)—he will acknowledge his error and ask God to forgive—and He will (1 John 1:9).

Through Worship a Person's Knowledge and Understanding of the Will of God Significantly Increases

Another blessing of true worship, and one which—without intending to minimize the value of the others—I consider to be among the most coveted, is that through it a person's knowledge and understanding of God's will significantly increases. When in the sphere of worship a person listens to God's word being read and carefully and thoroughly explained, his knowledge and understanding of it will naturally grow.

Why is increasing in the knowledge and understanding of God's will such a wonderful blessing? Simply put, because God has promised to bless eternally only those who do His will (i.e., His desires) (Matthew 7:21; 12:50; Luke 12:41-48; John 7:17; 9:31; Ephesians 6:6; Hebrews 10:36; 1 Peter 4:2; 1 John 2:17); and one cannot *do* His will—socially, morally, ethically, or religiously—without first *knowing* and *understanding* it (cf. Ezra 7:10). With this in mind, it is no wonder that Paul says to the church at Colossae, "We have not ceased to pray for you and to ask that you may be filled with the knowledge of His will . . ." (Colossians 1:9-10).

Through Worship a Person Receives Encouragement for Living the Christian Life

A final blessing of worship that I want to mention is that through it a person receives continued encouragement for Christian living. The Scriptures clearly teach that spiritual challenges, suffering, and hardship will frequently test the fidelity of those who choose to live for God (Matthew 5:11; 10:17,22,39; Acts 5:40-41; 14:22; Romans 8:16-18; 2 Corinthians 4:7-10; 2 Timothy 3:12; Hebrews 11:25, 32-40; 1

Peter 1:6; 4:12-14; 5:10). As a result, it is natural for a person to become emotionally weary and overwhelmed with discouragement at times throughout their walk of faith.

During these periods of deep discouragement and emotional fatigue, Christians need to be encouraged and inspired to keep fighting the "good fight of faith." They also need encouragement and inspiration when the periods of discouragement are not so deep. One way that a Christian receives needed encouragement and inspiration is through worship. In other words, God has so designed worship that it has a way of "re-charging" those who become emotionally drained from dealing with the "everyday" challenges, as well as the "not-so-everyday" challenges, associated with Christian living.

Of course, this is not to suggest that worship should be viewed merely or primarily as an occasion to "re-charge" one's emotional and spiritual batteries. To view worship this way would be to view it primarily as a self-serving event, and as was previously observed, to view worship primarily as a self-serving event makes man, not God, the center of worship and perverts its true meaning and purpose. To say that worship has a way of "re-charging" people is simply to acknowledge the fact that encouragement and emotional uplift often come to those who worship.

After death God will transform His disciples into physically, emotionally, intellectually, and spiritually perfect people. This is the destiny of those who remain faithful to God. The Scriptures often speak of this destiny and sometimes refer to it as "glory" (Romans 5:2; 8:17-18,23; Philippians 3:20-21; 1 John 3:2). With this in mind, could anyone seriously challenge the suggestion that Christians will often be encouraged and experience emotional uplift when, through worship, they are confronted with this destiny and meditate on it?

The Irony of All This

In this chapter I identified several potential blessings of true worship. There is, however, something of an irony in regard to the reception of these, or any other, personal blessings of worship. That irony is that these blessings will *fully* come only to those whose primary reason for worshiping is to give adoration and praise to God. I am convinced that they will not be fully received if one is worshiping largely to get some sort of personal reward or payoff. As C.S. Lewis observed, one cannot pursue "first things" ("seek ye first") in order to obtain "second things" ("all these things will be added").[4]

It is important to remember, however, that, as stated earlier, this does not mean that it is inappropriate to anticipate and desire the blessings of worship. It simply means that one should not worship primarily in order to receive personal rewards or blessings. What I am talking about here is priorities of motive.

Questions to Guide Study

1. What are some ways that knowing and understanding God will bless a person?

2. How does recognizing one's sinfulness bless a person?

3. What are the personal rewards of one's recognizing his great intrinsic value and the fact that God is genuinely interested in him or her?

4. How does being reminded of one's privileged position in Christ positively impact a person?

5. What will a person inevitably be confronted with in worship that will prompt him or her to view life from an eternal perspective? What are some benefits of viewing life from such a perspective?

6. Why is increasing in the knowledge and understanding of God's will a great blessing?

Endnotes

[1]Curtis Dickinson, "What's Happened to God?" *The Witness* (May 1976), 16:1.

[2]Ibid., 1-2.

[3]Jack Cottrell, *What the Bible Says About God the Redeemer* (Joplin, MO: College Press Publishing Co., 1987), 250.

[4]C.S. Lewis, "First and Second Things," *God in the Dock* (Grand Rapids: Eerdmans, 1970), 278-281.

Chapter 13
Activities in the Assembly[1]

One does not have to spend a great deal of time reading the New Testament to be impressed by the fact that early Christians frequently met together (Acts 4:31; 11:26; 14:27; 15:6; 20:7-8; 1 Corinthians 5:4; 11:17, 33-34; 14:26). As Everett Ferguson observes, "Christianity was not a private religious experience."[2]

One reason they gathered was so that they could minister to and encourage one another. As Ferguson notes,

> In community there is strength. Individual weaknesses are overcome through the encouragement of others. People need one another. And the meetings of the church provide the opportunity for learning of needs, planning to meet them, and acting together. Forsaking the assembly is not a sin against an institution, but against the brothers and sisters to whom we owe mutual edification and fellowship (Hebrews 10:25).[3]

The church, however, did not assemble only to encourage each other. Christians also gathered to approach and worship

God (Hebrews 10:19-25). We see the connection between the assembly and worship clearly in Hebrews 2:12. Here the inspired writer quotes from Psalm 22:22: "I will proclaim Thy name to My brethren, In the midst of the congregation I will sing Thy praise." We can also see the connection between the assembly and worship in Hebrews 12:23-28. Here the Hebrew writer connects the "assembly and church of the firstborn who are enrolled in heaven" with offering "to God an acceptable worship with reverence and awe."

As the church gathered each Lord's day for mutual edification and worship, there were certain activities that were a regular part of their meetings. In this chapter I will identify and discuss these activities.

The Lord's Supper

It seems logical to begin our discussion with the Lord's supper since it was the central act of the weekly assembly of the early church. As Ferguson puts it simply, "There were meetings to take the Lord's supper (1 Corinthians 11:20-21, 33), and these occurred on the first day of the week (Acts 20:7)."[4]

I think the best way to gain a proper understanding and appreciation of this weekly activity is to consider some of the terms which are associated with it in Scripture.

1) *Lord's Supper.* This is probably the most common term used in Protestant churches to identify this activity. This term reminds us that this activity is particularly and exclusively the Lord's. It is His supper (1 Corinthians 11:20), not our supper (1 Corinthians 11:21). It is His table (1 Corinthians 10:21), not our table. He sets the table for us. He invites us to the table. We are His guests. And He presides as we gather around the table. As we eat and drink at the table, we do so to His honor. When we speak of the Lord's supper, our attention is called to what God has given us—Jesus the Christ.

2) *Thanksgiving.* In all four accounts of Christ's instituting His supper the verb "give thanks" is used (Matthew 26:27; Mark 14:23; Luke 22:17; 1 Corinthians 11:24). The basis for

"giving thanks" is the salvation that brought the church into existence (the Greek word that is translated "give thanks" in these passages is *eucharisteo*. For this reason many have come to refer to the Lord's supper as the *eucharist*). When the church "gives thanks" for the bread and cup, we are thanking God for the salvation brought by the death and resurrection of Jesus, and our attention is called to what we give God.

3) *Communion*. This is a translation of the Greek word *koinonia* and is another common term for the Lord's supper (1 Corinthians 10:16-17. Sometimes *koinonia* in this context is translated *fellowship*, *sharing*, and *participation*). These terms call our attention to the mutual sharing, both with Christ and with one another, that characterizes the church.

In 1 Corinthians 10:14-21 Paul contends that, in some way, eating at idol temples establishes communion with demons. When we gather at the Lord's table and eat the unleavened bread and drink the fruit of the vine we are sharing in Christ's sacrifice and its benefits. We are participating in Christ's body and blood. We are identifying with His life and death. We are communing with Him.

Not only do we commune or share with Christ when we eat the Lord's supper, but we also commune and share with one another in this profound activity. Another term associated with the Lord's supper that really calls our attention to this fact is *break bread* (Acts 20:7). This term portrays the Lord's supper as a sharing of food together.

Table fellowship in the biblical world was something much different than what is usually conjured up in our twenty-first century minds when we think of table fellowship. In the biblical world it was a sign of extreme closeness and sharing. It said volumes about the relationship that existed between participants. As we break the one loaf (1 Corinthians 10:17), we proclaim that we are all of the same community, the same family. And as we eat the bread and drink the cup, we express the fact that we are united with and committed to one another, now and through eternity.

4) *Memorial.* Our sharing with Christ and our spiritual brothers and sisters is based on a past event. When we eat the Lord's supper, we commemorate and remember that past event—the death and resurrection of Christ. However, there must be more to remembering Christ's work than simply recalling past events. We need to remember it as the Jews remember the events of the exodus.

When Jews celebrate Passover, they see themselves as actually participating in the exodus. They are challenged to think of themselves not as being 3,500 years removed from the exodus, but as being the very ones that God brought out of Egypt. In other words, as they remember, they bring the past into the present. We must do no less as we eat the unleavened bread and drink the fruit of the vine. As I eat the bread and drink the cup, I must remember that Jesus died that day for me. I must understand that the Son of God had me in mind as His blood streamed from His body and puddled at the foot of the cross. I must remember that God was making a covenant with me on that day. The language of memorial calls us to consider what God has done and is doing for us.

Paul goes on to say that participating in this memorial of Jesus "proclaims His death" (1 Corinthians 11:26). In the Lord's supper we reenact the event that is the basis for our salvation—the death of Jesus. And in the Lord's supper we silently proclaim—a proclamation that is as loud as any words—that we believe Jesus died for us.

5) *Anticipation of future hope.* As we eat the Lord's supper, we do so "until He comes" (1 Corinthians 11:26). This language calls our attention to the fact that a glorious future goes with the past event of Christ's death, burial, and resurrection.

When we eat the Lord's supper, we not only bring the past into the present, but we also proclaim our confidence in that glorious future. So, in a sense, we also bring the future into the present. Our future sharing with Christ is so certain that we celebrate it now. When we eat the Lord's supper, our attention is not directed just to a past event, but also to our future hope that is guaranteed by that past event.

Question. If we really bring our future glory into the present as we eat the Lord's supper, should our observance of it always seem so sorrowful? Early Christian observances of the Lord's supper were generally characterized by a joyful tone; a tone that no doubt was shaped by their joyful expectation of one day sharing in Christ's glory. I think we make a mistake if our observance of this memorial feast always seems sad.

6) *Covenant meal.* In each recorded instance of Christ's instituting His supper, the text speaks of a "new covenant" in reference to the blood of Jesus. This language calls to our attention the fact that we belong to the Lord and that this meal is reserved for those who share the covenant.

When we drink from the cup, we share in this covenant of blood. The old covenant was inaugurated by sacrifice and the eating of a covenant meal (Exodus 24:3-11). For Christians, when we eat the bread and drink the cup we are renewing our covenant allegiance to the Lord. We are renewing a relationship that will not permit other religious loyalties (1 Corinthians 10:21). This meal is a physical and visible expression that we are in covenant with God. It is a silent declaration that we belong to Him.

How Shall We Eat?

First and foremost, as we come to the Lord's table, we must come with a correct understanding of the meaning and significance of the supper. That is, we must come with an understanding of the concepts discussed above. Of course this does not mean we need a perfect understanding of all these concepts before we can eat at Christ's table. It simply means that we need to know something about the meaning and significance of what we are putting into our mouths. And we need to be constantly growing in our understanding and appreciation of this uniquely Christian activity.

Beyond coming to the Lord's table with an understanding and appreciation of what it means, Paul calls us to "examine" ourselves (1 Corinthians 11:28). In context, this call may primarily be a call to examine our relationship with our brothers and sisters; but surely a wider application is permissible.

Just before he tells us to examine ourselves, Paul speaks of eating and drinking "in an unworthy manner" (1 Corinthians 11:27). Note the word *manner*. This is not talking about our worthiness to eat the supper. None of us are worthy of God's grace; that is why, as many have observed, it is grace. None of us are worthy of what God has done in Christ. And none of us are worthy to be the Lord's guest at His table. We come to Christ's table because we are spiritually impoverished without Christ. With this in mind, it seems that eating the Lord's supper "in an unworthy manner" must mean, in part, eating it without a conscious appreciation of the fact that we are unworthy sinners who stand in need of mercy and forgiveness. Surely those who come to the Lord's table with a heart full of arrogance and self-righteousness will eat in an unworthy manner.

In addition to self-examination, other attitudes and spiritual exercises are certainly appropriate as we eat at Christ's table. One such spiritual exercise is *confession*. When we examine ourselves and find ourselves desperate for forgiveness, we will naturally be led to a confession of our sins. As *we* witness the cross in our mind's eye, we will be reminded of just why He had to go to the cross—it was because of *our* sins. This awareness will prompt nothing less than a full confession.

Another attitude that should prevail at Christ's table is an attitude of *reconciliation*. This activity is a community activity. It is not just personal, private communion. As we reflect on this, we must make every effort to come to the supper in peaceful harmony with our fellow partakers—our brothers and sisters. Consequently, our thoughts at this time will not be solely on the past work of Christ and our future glory. We will also have loving thoughts and prayers for those with whom we are sharing this meal.

A fourth attitude or spiritual exercise that is appropriate as we eat the Lord's supper is *rededication*. As we celebrate, by eating this meal, the fact that we are in covenant with God, we are always led to renew our dedication and loyalty to God. Our loyalty to Him simply will not permit associations with things that are sinful (1 Corinthians 10:21).

A final attitude that is proper and appropriate in connection with the Lord's supper is *joy*. As we relive the events that guarantee our glorious future, and as we anticipate the end of time which will usher in that glorious future, joy will be a natural response.

When Shall We Eat?

Within churches in the Restoration Movement, discussion of the Lord's supper has always gone beyond its meaning and significance to include the question, "When and how often should Christians observe the Lord's supper?" I believe such a question is rightfully asked and must be considered. In fact, no perspective on the Lord's supper will be complete until this question is asked and answered.

Where shall we go to find a satisfactory answer to this question? Church tradition? Hardly. How about church history? Not quite, although a study of church history is beneficial because it allows us to test our understanding of the New Testament against the understanding of the earliest churches outside the New Testament (Of course, there are other good reasons to study church history as well).

It behooves us as New Testament Christians to examine the inspired, apostolic record for guidance on this matter. And as we explore the text, we find that, although there are no direct commands regarding the time when the church should gather around the Lord's table, there are clear indications of when it was done.

Relying solely on the Biblical record, one discovers that the early church clearly met on the first day of every week to eat this covenant meal. The clearest indication of this is Luke's statement in Acts 20:7: "On the first day of the week, when we were gathered together to break bread, Paul began talking to them, intending to leave the next day, and he prolonged his message until midnight."

Another passage that will help us in this matter is 1 Corinthians 11:20-21, 33. This passage clearly shows that the church at Corinth was meeting together primarily in order to eat the Lord's supper. How does this help us in the matter of determining when we shall eat it? Well, 1 Corinthians 16:2 clearly suggests that the church was assembling every Lord's day. When the information from these two passages is considered together, the logical conclusion is that they were gathering every Lord's day (1 Corinthians 16:2) for the primary purpose of eating the Lord's supper (1 Corinthians 11:20-21, 33).

Since there is, as we have just seen, clear biblical precedent for the matter of when the Lord's supper shall be eaten, I am convinced that we must confine our eating to this time. Interestingly enough, church history also testifies that a weekly celebration of this feast continued for at least two centuries after Christ's church was established.

If I had to sum up my conclusion on this matter I would probably express it much as George R. Beasley-Murray does. Dr. Murray is an internationally known British scholar and, interestingly enough, a Baptist. I say "interestingly enough" because he has some rather "un-Baptist" views of things (at least they would be considered "un-Baptist" by the most Baptists in the United States). When asked about his views concerning the Lord's supper, Murray said, "My own views as a young preacher speedily led me to the conviction that the primitive New Testament pattern of the weekly observance was there and that there was every reason to follow it."[5] Is that not refreshing?—we eat the Lord's supper each Lord's day just because that is the example we find in Scripture.

What shall we say to those who refuse to follow the New Testament precedent for eating the Lord's supper each first day of the week? With charity and kindness I must remind them that there is no Biblical warrant for any other practice. And since there is no Biblical warrant for any other practice,

I must tell them that it is impossible to know whether or not God will be offended by any other practice. Since we cannot know for certain whether or not God will be offended by any other practice, with charity and kindness I must tell them that, as Batsell Barrett Baxter said, "It is a wise, safe course to do it as the early Christians did, not annually, not semi-annually, not quarterly, not monthly, but on each Lord's Day."[6]

Prayer

Even a cursory reading of the New Testament clearly shows that prayer was a central feature when the church gathered (Acts 2:42; Acts 4:24-31; 12:5, 12; 1 Corinthians 14:14-15; 1 Timothy 2:1-2). Although most features of congregational prayer are the same as private prayer, the group setting, as Ferguson notes, "gives a distinctive color to the prayers."[7]

Those who lead an assembly of the church in prayer are not praying a personal, private prayer in public. The church is not "listening in" to someone's private prayer. The leader is standing before God as the congregation's representative, and he is voicing the concerns of the entire body. The congregation is actually praying. The leader is simply leading the thoughts and giving expression to them. The practice of the whole church saying "amen" at the close of a public prayer (1 Corinthians 14:16) is an indication that the words which were spoken comprised a corporate act. It indicates that it was an act of the whole body, an expression of the whole people, an expression of unity.

In Jesus' Name

Although our prayers as Christians have much in common with the prayers of Old Testament saints, our prayers as Christians are distinct from theirs. The primary distinction between our prayers and theirs is that ours are done with reference to Christ. The apostle John connects prayer with the name of Jesus (John 14:13-14; 15:16; 16:24, 26). Jesus said prayer is "in my name." So, as we Christians pray, we must do so in Jesus' name.

What does it mean to pray "in Jesus' name"? Does it simply mean we must end our prayers with that phrase? Not exactly. To pray "in the name of Jesus" or "in Jesus' name" is not a formula which Christians are required to verbalize when they pray. It is a belief. It is a conviction. In other words, one can be praying "in the name of Jesus" without actually verbalizing those words.

To pray in the name of Jesus means that as we pray, we do so as one who believes that Jesus is the son of God and the savior of the world. It means we pray as one who believes that only through and because of Christ can we approach God and commune with Him. It means we pray as one who is committed to the mission of Christ. It means we pray as one who recognizes and respects Christ's authority. It means we pray as one who is submissive to Christ's will. And it means we pray as one who seeks to bring glory and honor to Christ—as one who seeks to set Christ forward.

Having said that praying "in the name of Christ" is not a formula which must be recited when we pray (there is neither a specific command to do so, or a Biblical example of such a recital being done), I am strongly committed to verbalizing it when I pray, and I am strongly committed to encouraging others to verbalize it when they pray. Why? Because it is a powerful, regular verbal reminder to ourselves and the congregation we lead about how we come before the throne of God—we come because of Christ, through Christ, in union with Christ, and committed to Christ.

An Intimate Meeting With God

Our commitment to prayer is rooted in the example and teaching of Jesus. Messiah had a passionate and committed prayer life while on the earth (Luke 3:21; 4:42-43; 5:16; 6:12; 9:18; 9:29; 22:31-32; 22:39-46; 23:34, 46). His pattern of prayer prompted His disciples to ask Him to teach them how to pray. His response resulted in what we call "the model prayer" (Luke 11:1-4). Also, as we consider the subject of Jesus and prayer, we must not overlook the fact that He taught several parables about prayer (Luke 11:5-13; 18:1-14).

Since we are in Christ and share in His Sonship (Galatians 3:26), we have the wonderful privilege of addressing God as Christ did, as Father. In fact, Jesus Himself taught His disciples to address God in this way (Luke 11:2). The glorious truth is that we enjoy the same intimate and open approach to God that Jesus enjoyed.

As we talk about our open and intimate approach to God, I feel it is important to say that this aspect of our relationship in no way obscures or detracts from God's sovereignty over all things. In other words, calling God Father does not imply easy familiarity with Him. It does not suggest that we are approaching Him without reverence and awe. We approach Him intimately and openly, while at the same time we approach Him with reverence and awe. Intimacy and openness are not incompatible with reverence and awe.

The Components of Prayer

One of the most popular ways of expressing the various components or parts of prayer is with the acronym ACTS: Adoration, Confession, Thanksgiving, and Supplication. Although not in the same order, these parts of prayer basically correspond to the elements in Jesus' model prayer (i.e., the Lord's prayer—Matthew 6:9-13). Of course, not every prayer will contain all these elements. Some prayers may focus almost exclusively on one element.

1) *Adoration.* Prayer is one way we express praise to God. As one reads the Psalms, he will begin to see that praises of God were sometimes descriptive (God is) while at other times they were narrative (God does). In the same way, in our prayers as Christians we may sometimes praise God for who He is (1 Timothy 6:15-16), while at other times we may praise Him for what He has done (Acts 4:24-26; Ephesians 1:3ff). The model prayer begins with an expression that may

be understood as an expression of praise and adoration: "Our Father who is in heaven, Hallowed be Your name."

2) *Confession*. Confession has two prongs. First of all, in prayer we confess our faith in God. Second, in prayer we confess our sins to God. As Ferguson notes, "They are related."[8] When we confess who God is, and confess our faith in Him, we are made aware of the moral difference between us and God—He is complete moral and ethical perfection, and we are sinners. Likewise, when we confess our sins to God, the way to forgiveness and greater faith is opened. The model prayer opens with a confession of who God is and concludes with pleas that God will forgive us and deliver us from the power of the evil one.

3) *Thanksgiving*. As we thank God, we get specific and personal in our prayers. Although in this form thanksgiving is lacking from the model prayer, it is very characteristic of Paul's prayers. Without being exhaustive, Paul gave thanks to God for His grace (1 Corinthians 1:4), for His indescribable gift (2 Corinthians 9:15), for deliverance from death (Romans 7:25), for food (1 Corinthians 10:30), for all things (Ephesians 5:20), for churches—for various reasons (Romans 1:8; Colossians 1:4-5; 1 Thessalonians 2:13; Philippians 1:3-5; 2 Corinthians 9:11-12; Romans 15:13), and his missionary work was a special concern of prayer (Romans 10:1; Colossians 4:3; 2 Thessalonians 3:1).

4) *Supplication*. Supplications are petitions we make to God. In other words, it is calling on God to do something for us. We not only thank Him for His gifts, but we make our requests known to Him (Philippians 4:6). From beginning to end, Scripture presents a picture of men and women asking God to intervene in human affairs and give them the desires of their hearts.

Although the petitions of the model prayer focus on spiritual concern and needs (the kingdom and will of God and deliverance from temptation and sin), there are included petitions for physical needs—"give us this day our daily bread" (Matthew 6:11).

As we contemplate the privilege of petitioning God, we must keep in mind the importance of petitioning Him on behalf of others—for their welfare (physical as well as spiritual). John prayed that his friend Gaius might "prosper and be in good health, just as your soul prospers" (3 John 2). This dimension of petitionary prayer keeps foremost in our minds the fact that we are a community of Christians committed to and concerned about the welfare of each other. This dimension of petitionary prayer reflects the "one another-ness" of Christianity.

Singing

Like prayer, singing in the early church was an activity that belonged not only to daily religious life, but also to the assembly. Several passages make it clear that when believers gathered, they sang (Matthew 26:30; Ephesians 5:19; Colossians 3:16-17[9]; 1 Corinthians 14:15, 26).

Also like prayer, the distinctiveness of Christian singing is that it is done "in the name of our Lord Jesus Christ" (Ephesians 5:19-20; Colossians 3:16-17). As with prayer, to sing in the name of Jesus means that we sing as one who believes that Jesus is the Son of God and the savior of the world. It means we sing as one who believes that only through and because of Christ can we approach and commune with God. It means we sing as one who is committed to the mission of Christ. It means we sing as one who recognizes and respects Christ's authority. It means we sing as one who is submissive to Christ's will. And it means we sing as one who seeks, above all things, to bring glory and honor to Christ.

A Theology of Singing

How should we understand and view Christian singing—both in a private, personal context and in a public context? The Scriptures provide us with a rich understanding of this wonderful activity.

1) *Singing is a way of preaching Christ.* Much of our singing should be about Christ. The early hymns that have been

identified in the New Testament are about Christ (e.g., Philippians 2:6-11; 1 Timothy 3:16). When we as the body of Christ sing about Him, we are in a very real sense preaching Him to all who have gathered.

2) *Singing is a confession of faith.* In ancient times, singing was closely related to prayer (cf. 1 Corinthians 14:15; James 5:13). Therefore, the same components of prayer which were noted earlier—adoration, confession, thanksgiving, and supplication—are just as applicable to singing.

Recognizing these attributes, we understand that singing is a way that we acknowledge (i.e., confess) God. Hebrews 13:15 uses a word (*homologeo*—usually translated "give thanks" in this verse) that can be translated "confess" or "acknowledge" (cf. Matthew 10:32; Luke 12:8; John 9:22; Romans 10:9; 1 John 1:9; 4:3; Revelation 3:5). Here's how the Amplified Version translates the verse: "Through Him therefore let us constantly and at all times offer up to God a sacrifice of praise, which is the fruit of lips that thankfully acknowledge and confess and glorify His name."

In the Psalms this idea of confessing or acknowledging God is often connected with singing. For instance, Psalm 18:49, which is quoted in Romans 15:9, says, "Therefore I will give thanks to You among the nations, O Lord, And I will sing praises to Your name." When Paul quotes this psalm in Romans 15:9, he uses the word *homologeo*. Here's how the King James version translates Paul's words: ". . . For this cause I will confess to thee among the Gentiles, and sing unto thy name."

3) *Singing is an expression of thanks.* Ephesians 5:19 exhorts us to speak "to one another in psalms and hymns and spiritual songs, singing and making melody with your heart to the Lord; always giving thanks for all things in the name of our Lord Jesus Christ to God, even the Father." Similarly, Colossians 3:16 says, "Let the word of Christ richly dwell within you, with all wisdom teaching and admonishing one another with psalms and hymns and spiritual songs, singing with thankfulness in your hearts to God." When we sing

with thankfulness in our hearts, verbalizing that thanks will be natural.

4) *Singing expresses the presence of the Holy Spirit and the Word of Christ.* Ephesians 5:18-19 associates singing with being filled with the Spirit, and Colossians 3:16 associates singing with the indwelling Word of Christ. As Ferguson says,

> Both statements are true and belong together; singing is the result of the presence of the Spirit and of the Word of Christ. Praise is the consequence of being filled with the Spirit and possessing the word of Christ. When the Spirit and the Word of Christ dwells in a person, it finds expression in song. The knowledge of salvation in Christ, the acceptance of God's grace, the receiving of the Holy Spirit as the firstfruits of redemption—this leads to song.[10]

5) *Singing praise is a spiritual sacrifice.* The New Testament connects singing with the Spirit (1 Corinthians 14:15) and speaks of "spiritual songs" (Ephesians 5:19; Colossians 3:16). When members of the body of Christ sing together, we are engaged in a spiritual activity. We are making a spiritual offering to God. Singing is one of the offerings that, for Christians, replace the sacrifices which were a part of the Old Testament sacrificial system. And this offering is one which is continually available for the Christian.

6) *Singing is a sharing in heavenly praise.* Heavenly beings are constantly praising God in song (Revelation 4:8, 10-11; 5:8-12; 14:2-3; 15:2-3). When we Christians sing, we join this wonderful heavenly chorus. And as we do so, the barriers between heaven and earth, and time and eternity, are lowered for a moment.

7) *Singing is for mutual edification.* While I would suggest that singing in the assembly should primarily be directed to God, it is impossible to escape the fact that it is also directed to one another for teaching and admonition. Paul contends in Colossians 3:16 that singing is a vehicle of instruction. In other words, teaching occurs through song. (Even if

Paul intended for "teaching and admonishing" to be taken separately from "singing" in this passage, it is still closely parallel to it.)

Furthermore, in 1 Corinthians 14:26 the Holy Spirit commands that everything done in our assemblies must be done with a view toward edifying the church community. Since edification requires understanding what is said (1 Corinthians 14:9, 16-17, 19), the melody of a song must always be considered secondary to the words. The melody of a song must support the ideas expressed in a song. It must never overshadow the message of a song.

8) *Singing promotes and exemplifies the unity of the church.* When the church, with one voice, glorifies God, it expresses and symbolizes its oneness. It is a display of oneness with Christ and each other. Singing also helps to bring about unity among believers. There is something about singing together that gives those involved a sense of common identity and promotes solidarity.

9) *Singing expresses deep religious emotion.* Music adds to the emotional impact of what is being expressed in a song. It is the language of the soul. It brings about an emotional release. That is, it can express better and more fully than words alone the deep feelings in our hearts. James said, "Are any cheerful? They should sing songs of praise" (James 5:13).

Giving

As I read the New Testament, particularly the book of Acts, I cannot help but be impressed by the constant willingness and readiness to give that characterized so many first century Christians (Acts 2:44-45; 4:32-37; 6:1-7; 2 Corinthians 8:1-6). This same readiness and willingness to give should be a constant feature of our lives (Romans 12:13; James 2:14-17). Giving, however, is done not only as a private activity, but as a corporate action through the church (Acts 4:34-35; 11:29-30). Paul refers to this corporate, public activity in 1 Corinthians 16:1 when he says, "Now concerning the collection . . ." As many have observed, this passage contains at least five principles concerning public giving.

1) *It is to be a universal practice.* For one thing, giving is to be done in every church. Paul's instruction to the church at Corinth was, do "as I directed the churches of Galatia" (1 Corinthians 16:1). Whether you gather on the Lord's day with a church in Nashville, Tennessee, or with one in London, England, you can be rest assured that a collection will be taken—just as one was taken in the churches in Galatia and in the church at Corinth twenty centuries ago.

2) *It is to be a weekly practice.* Paul's command to the churches of Galatia and Corinth was to give "on the first day of every week" (1 Corinthians 16:2). Just as important as it was to break bread when the church assembled each first day of the week (Acts 20:7), was the offering of a financial gift to meet legitimate needs of the church.

3) *It is to be a personal act.* Who is to give? Paul says, ". . . let each one of you . . ." (1 Corinthians 16:2). Every Christian has the responsibility to give. Christian parents should teach their children this principle early in life. Even if their contribution is only a few pennies, children need to learn that giving is not only a privilege and joy, but also a personal responsibility.

4) *It is to be a predetermined amount.* Paul taught, "put aside and save . . ." (1 Corinthians 16:2). What we give to God should be determined in advance. When we assemble on the Lord's day, we should have already given thought to, and determined, the amount we will offer. This is not said to discourage spontaneous giving. As we all know, needs sometimes arise which may require a spontaneous gift.

Why is it so important to predetermine what we will give? Well, for one thing, and most importantly, God commands it. So, obedience to God requires it. Beyond this, I can really only speculate. But I would suggest that giving prior thought to what we will give God forces us—at least it should—to spend some time reflecting deeply on our relationship with God and on what He has given us. This kind of deep reflection should ensure that our giving is not simply a spur-of-the-moment leftover, but rather a generous, well-thought-out expression of gratitude and devotion.

5) *It is to be a proportional act.* Paul also taught that a person's giving should be "as he may prosper" (1 Corinthians 16:2). What exactly does this mean? Is it legislating a certain percentage of our income? Of course we all probably know that many of our religious friends and neighbors legislate that a tithe be given to God. While a tithe was the minimum amount the Jews were commanded to give (Leviticus 27:30-33), the New Testament does not legislate a percentage of income to give. Therefore, it would be improper for us to legislate one.

Nevertheless, it is my personal *opinion*—as it is the opinion of many—that ten percent is a pretty good place for Christians to start their giving. Am I not afraid that, if consistently practiced, giving only ten percent may reduce what people are presently giving to God? First of all, I did not say that I was of the opinion that Christians should give *only* ten percent. I said that I am of the opinion that ten percent is a good place *to start.* Second, not only do I *not* think that any church's contribution will go down if everyone starts giving a minimum of ten percent, I am quite confident that if all Christians would give God a minimum of ten percent of their after-tax income, churches would have more money than ever before to use in kingdom matters.

Giving Is . . .

The most extended discussion on giving in the New Testament occurs in 2 Corinthians 8-9. Here Paul is urging the Corinthian Christians to complete what they had promised to give for the relief of their brethren in Judea (2 Corinthians 8:1-6, 10-11). From these chapters we learn much about giving.

1) *Giving is a privilege.* Referring to the Macedonian brethren Paul said, "For I testify that according to their ability, and beyond their ability they gave of their own accord, begging us with much entreaty for the *favor* of participation in the support of the saints" (2 Corinthians 8:3-4). Another

way of translating the word *favor* is *privilege* (NIV). God's people should never view giving as a obligation to be endured, but rather as a privilege to be enjoyed and anticipated. It is a privilege to give because it is a privilege to show the grace and goodness of God to others. It is a privilege to give because it is a privilege to express thanks to God for His "indescribable gift" (2 Corinthians 9:15).

2) *Giving is an act of fellowship.* Paul says that the Macedonians begged him to *participate* (i.e., share) in the ministry of support for the saints. When we give money to the work of the Lord we are sharing in a very special way with those who do likewise. We are expressing our unity to Christ and each other. The historical context of 2 Corinthians 8-9 made the contribution of the Gentile churches for Jewish brothers and sisters a very important expression of Christian unity.

3) *Giving is a ministry.* When the Macedonians gave, they were involved in a ministry, a service (2 Corinthians 8:4; 2 Corinthians 9:1). All Christians are to be involved in ministry, in serving others. Giving is one way of ministering to others.

4) *Giving is a test or proof.* Since the gospel is the story of God's giving, our giving is a test or proof of our response to the gospel. It is a proof of our obedience. It is a proof of our confession of the gospel (2 Corinthians 9:13). It is something of a barometer of our interest in the kingdom of God. The Macedonian Christians passed the test (2 Corinthians 8:2); now it was being applied to the Corinthian Christians (2 Corinthians 9:13).

Reading and Preaching the Scriptures

Delivering and receiving the word of God are also important features of a church's public assembly. Timothy was told by Paul, "Until I come, give attention to the public reading of Scripture, to exhortation and teaching" (1 Timothy 4:12). 1 Corinthians 14, our clearest Biblical picture of a Christian assembly, shows the prominent place that delivering the word of God occupied in these gatherings.

Here Paul refers to the activities of prophesying, teaching, speaking in tongues, and interpreting those tongues (1 Corinthians 14:26). Each of these activities was a vehicle for bringing the word of God to the ears of those present.

Hearing the word of the Lord makes us aware of God's presence in the assembly and thus is an important part of the worship experience. Furthermore, it is largely through hearing and understanding God's word that we are blessed by the worship experience. It is through hearing and understanding God's word that we are, as Paul argues, edified, built up, or strengthened (1 Corinthians 14:19, 26).

The church is a people called by the word of the Lord. That word continues to call us together in assembly. Through the reading and preaching of Scripture, that word continues to call out to us in the assembly.

A Word About Preaching

The Scriptures which contain the word and will of God must continue to be proclaimed and taught when God's people gather. The Scriptures must be interpreted and applied so that Christians can reach their fullest spiritual potential.

Given this fact, it is my opinion that the basic form of preaching heard in Christian gatherings should be expository sermons. Basically, an expository sermon is a detailed interpretation of a particular text and a practical application of it. It is explaining a text and relating it to the spiritual needs of listeners.

I am certainly not suggesting that "topical sermons" should be done away with. There are times when a topical sermon may "work best." But in the regular assembly, when God's people have gathered to hear the word of the Lord among other things, I believe expository preaching best accomplishes this goal. The preacher who faithfully interprets and applies a text in the assembly is bringing the word of God to people. He is truly a spokesman of God and so, as Ferguson says, "has an awesome task."[11]

Questions to Guide Study

1. Identify some of the terms which are associated with the Lord's supper in Scripture and discuss their significance (i.e., what do these terms tell us about the Lord's supper?).

2. What Biblical evidence exists to help us answer the question, "When and how often shall we eat at Christ's table?"

3. What are some attitudes and "spiritual exercises" that are appropriate for one who is eating the Lord's supper?

4. What does it mean to pray in Jesus' name?

5. Describe the leader's role in public prayer.

6. Identify and discuss the components of prayer.

7. What are some of the Biblical texts which show singing to be a part of Christian gatherings?

8. Identify some of the things that are accomplished through singing.

9. Identify and discuss five principles for giving that are found in 1 Corinthians 16:1-2.

10. How is giving an act of fellowship?

11. How do you feel about the assertion that giving is a reflection of one's interest in spiritual matters? Do you agree or disagree? Explain your answer.

12. Read 1 Timothy 4:12. Why is it so important that reading Scripture and preaching maintain a prominent place in Christian assemblies?

Endnotes

[1]This title is borrowed from Everett Ferguson's book *The Church of Christ: A Biblical Ecclesiology for Today* (Grand Rapids: Eerdmans, 1996), 247. I must also point out that the content of this chapter is essentially a summary of brother Ferguson's discussion. For an expanded discussion of "activities in the assembly," I highly recommend that readers consult brother Ferguson's work.

[2]Everett Ferguson, *The Church of Christ: A Biblical Ecclesiology for Today* (Grand Rapids: Eerdmans, 1996), 233.

[3]Ibid.

[4]Ibid., 249-250.

[5]"A British Baptist Speaks," an interview of George R. Beasley-Murray by John A. Owston in *One Body* (Spring 1991): 19.

[6]Batsell Barrett Baxter, *Family of God: A Study of the New Testament Church* (Nashville, TN: Gospel Advocate Co., 1980): 117.

[7]Ferguson, 262.

[8]Ibid., 267.

[9]Although the literary setting or context of Ephesians 5:19 and Colossians 3:16-17 is the Christian life in a larger sense, Paul is using something from Christian assemblies—singing—to reinforce his point.

[10]Everett Ferguson, "The Theology of Singing," in *Harding College Lectures* (Austin, TX: Firm Foundation Publishing House, 1978), p. 79.

[11]Ferguson, *The Church of Christ*, 279.

Chapter 14
Inspiration Without Entertainment

Since Scripture most often presents worship as an occasion filled with joy and happiness, and at the same time always full of reverence and awe, can anyone really blame worshipers for expressing concern and general dissatisfaction when services seem to be little more than cold, uninspired ritual? Can anyone really blame them for leaving congregations where stale, lifeless services are the norm and going in search of worship that is more vibrant and meaningful? Can anyone really blame them for not eagerly anticipating worship if worship is, week after week, tired, listless, and unchallenging? And does anyone really believe that worshipers who have attended a stale, lifeless service will be filled with reverence and awe, gratitude and wonder, and be inspired to worship and serve God more faithfully?

Earlier I suggested that constant exposure to entertainment-styled services may actually destroy a person's appetite for real worship. I now want to suggest that constant exposure to services which are stale and lifeless may also destroy a person's appetite for worship—at least for *pub-*

lic worship. And unfortunately, week after week, in far too many churches, worship is indeed stale and lifeless.

What can churches do to ensure that their public services are vibrant, meaningful, and inspirational periods of praising and honoring God—while staying, of course, within the framework of Scripture and without framing worship as entertainment? This question has been asked numerous times in recent years, and many people have offered some very helpful suggestions. In this chapter I will restate what I believe to be some of the more helpful suggestions which have been offered.[1]

Public Scripture Reading

Many congregations need to renew their commitment to reading Scripture publicly when they assemble for worship. In far too many churches there is no regular public reading of Scripture, or it has been reduced simply to reading a few verses before the sermon. As one writer recently observed, "The Word of God deserves a stronger voice in our midst."

Why should the public reading of Scripture be a central feature of our worship assemblies? In short, because the Scriptures reveal what no other book does. They reveal the infinitely just, infinitely holy, and infinitely loving God. The Word reveals the Son of God and the savior of the world. And it reveals everything we need to know to reach our fullest spiritual potential and please the only true and living God. In other words, it is only through Scripture that we encounter, come to know, and grow in the Lord. With this in mind, it is no wonder Paul told Timothy, "Until I come, give attention to the public reading of Scripture, to exhortation and teaching" (1 Timothy 4:13).

Some may think that longer public readings of Scripture are largely unnecessary since much of our time together is spent listening to the Word of God being preached. In response to this suggestion, one should note that both preaching *and* Scripture reading were central features of first century assemblies (1 Timothy 4:13; Colossians 4:16; 1 Thessalonians 5:27). Since the apostles obviously saw the value and need for both, so should we. Preaching, while it is and must remain an important part of Christian gatherings, must not take the place of simply reading God's word when we gather. As one writer said, "The church needs a steady, strong diet of God's Word, both read and preached."

Others may think that longer public readings of Scripture are largely unnecessary since most Americans own at least one copy of the Bible and are literate enough to read it for themselves. While Scripture is certainly more available now than it has ever been, it seems that Americans in general are actually reading less of it than ever before. If this is true, the need for longer public readings of Scripture would seem to be greater now than ever before in this country. Furthermore, how can we convince people that they need to immerse themselves privately in the Word of God if all we do publicly is sprinkle them with it?

Here are some suggestions which have been offered to increase and enhance our efforts to read God's Word publicly:

1) *Begin worship with a reading from the Word of God.* A well-chosen reading from Scripture is a great way to prepare one's heart and mind for worship. How does it do this? For one thing, a well-chosen and well-read portion of Scripture can inspire awe and reverence within a person by calling his attention to the nature and work of God. The Psalms are especially well suited to begin a service; they magnify the nature and work of God in a very inspiring way.

2) *Occasionally devote an entire service to reading the Word of God.* Some congregations have a regular cycle of Sunday evening services when they read sections of Scripture, usually focusing on a particular theme, and interpose these readings with selected songs and prayers. Sometimes a congregation may even want to have a single lengthy reading as a focal point of a service. For instance, listening to the first three chapters of Genesis read in a way that makes it come to life can be as powerful as any sermon on the creation and fall of man.

3) *Establish a regular cycle of publicly reading through the entire Bible.* Reading through the entire Bible publicly is a great goal that many churches may want to consider. Some churches may want to devise their own scheme or systematic plan for doing this, while others may want to use what is called a lectionary to guide their readings. A lectionary, which can be found in many Christian bookstores, is basically a suggested sequence of readings from every portion of Scripture. If the suggested sequence of a lectionary is followed, a congregation will read through the Bible every three years.

4) *Occasionally engage the entire congregation in unison and responsive readings from Scripture.* Historically, this practice is centuries old in the Christian community, but seldom utilized in our fellowship. In a responsive reading, a leader reads a verse to the congregation, and the congregation responds by reading the refrain in unison. An excellent example of a passage which lends itself to responsive reading is Psalm 136. Each verse in this psalm is followed by the refrain, "For His lovingkindness is everlasting."

I find the idea of unison and responsive readings appealing for a couple of reasons. For one thing, when people are actually participating in a reading, they are more likely to pay closer attention to what is being read. Second, unison and responsive readings increase a congregation's direct participation in the worship service; and as stated earlier, I am very open to changes in public worship that increase a congregation's direct participation in it.

5) *Select good readers to publicly read Scripture.* I am convinced that poor reading is an obstacle to "listening to God." I believe that a poor reader is often the one thing that separates a meaningful, inspirational reading from one that is uninspired and less than meaningful. Most people would probably agree that it is very difficult to stay focused on and be inspired by a reading from God's Word if it is being read by someone who, among other things, mumbles or speaks too softly, mispronounces and stumbles over words, pauses in the wrong places, or never inflects his voice.

As many have observed, most congregations would never think of asking just anyone to lead singing or preach. Neither should just anyone be called on to read Scripture to the church. Church leaders need to be sensitive to the fact that God has equipped some people with the talent and ability to read publicly, just as He has equipped some people with the talent and ability to preach or lead singing publicly.

The Lord's Supper

I strongly believe that the Lord's supper should be the focal point of our Lord's day assemblies. Unfortunately, week after week, in far too many churches, this important Christian ceremony is rushed through with little to nothing said about its meaning or significance. In many churches, not only is nothing ever said when the Lord's supper is served, but even the prayers offered in connection with it are trite, reflecting little thought. It is tragic, not to mention less than meaningful, when the Lord's supper has the appearance of a dull ritual.

Why should so much time and attention be given to the Lord's supper? For one thing, it expresses the central realities of the Christian faith. It expresses the reality that Jesus of Nazareth was the Son of God and that He became flesh and blood. It expresses the reality that Jesus' body was broken and His blood was shed and that He was buried and rose again. It expresses the reality that His blood is the power that cleanses sin and that it reconciles people to God (i.e., changes their relationship with Him from one characterized by hostility to one characterized by friendship). It expresses the reality that every person can receive cleansing only through Christ's blood. And it expresses the reality that one day Jesus will return and His people will share the likeness of His glory.

In addition to expressing the realities of the Christian faith, the Lord's supper also expresses, as one writer said, "what the church is all about." It expresses the fact that, as noted earlier, we are united with and committed to Christ;

and it expresses the fact that we are united with and committed to one another, now and through eternity.

Here are some practical suggestions which have been offered to improve our efforts around the Lord's table and to restore the Lord's supper to its rightful place in our assemblies:

1) *Take enough time for the Lord's supper.* It is virtually impossible fully to appreciate the meaning and significance of the Lord's supper if it is rushed through. As one writer said, "It takes time to look backward, inward, outward, forward, and upward."

2) *Incorporate thought-provoking comments and readings around the Lord's table.* The meaning and significance of the Lord's supper should be brought to a congregation's attention every week with thought-provoking comments and readings. The risk of the Lord's supper becoming a dull, uninspired, meaningless ritual significantly increases as thought-provoking verbal reflections on its meaning and significance decrease.

I would also add that creativity and freshness in one's readings and comments will enhance most efforts around the Lord's table. If the comments and readings around the Lord's table are the same week after week, many worshipers may stop listening and thinking and simply start going through the motions as they eat the supper.

3) *Carefully select those who will lead the congregation in eating the Lord's supper.* Church leaders should be sensitive to people's talents, abilities, and spiritual commitment as they select men to lead the congregation in eating the Lord's supper. If at all possible, they should select men who have demonstrated some ability and desire to direct a congregation in observing the Lord's supper in meaningful, thought-provoking ways.

4) *Occasionally focus an entire service on the Lord's supper.* Occasionally a congregation may want to build an entire service around the Lord's supper. In such a service the songs, prayers, readings, and sermon would all emphasize the meaning and significance of this meal. This would not only

be very meaningful, but it would also emphasize the importance of the Lord's supper in the life of the church.

5) *Give attention to the prayers offered at the Lord's table.* Church leaders need to encourage men to give careful thought to the prayers they offer in connection with the Lord's supper. All too often prayers around the Lord's table are trite and predictable. As a result, they do little to promote deep reflection and appreciation for what the supper expresses and represents. The Lord's supper will be much more meaningful when careful forethought is given to the prayers offered in connection with it.

Public Prayers

Church leaders need to encourage those who lead public prayers to put careful thought and preparation into their prayers. Week after week, in far too many churches, public prayers reflect little or no forethought and preparation. Instead, they often seem to be recited from memory and filled with generalities and overused clichés and expressions. This can create the impression that they are being offered simply to fulfill some sort of obligation to have a public prayer. Few things are less inspiring and less meaningful.

Leading people to the throne of God is both a great privilege and a serious responsibility. Those who are given this responsibility need to understand and appreciate the fact that they are actually speaking to God on behalf of the entire congregation. That is, they are standing before God as the congregation's representative, and they are voicing to Him the congregation's corporate concerns, not their personal, private concerns. Careful thought and preparation are essential to accomplishing this feat effectively and meaningfully.

Here are some suggestions which have been offered to improve and enhance our corporate prayers:

1) *Consider writing out and reading more public prayers.* Although extemporaneous, spontaneous prayers will continue to be the norm in most public worship settings, many men would benefit from writing out their prayers, or at least

outlining them, before leading them. This suggestion is really about putting sufficient thought and preparation into public prayers.

As many have noted, few things are less inspiring and less meaningful than a spontaneous prayer that is shallow and full of generalities. At the same time, few things are more inspiring and more meaningful than a prayer that is obviously heart-felt and full of thought.

While some men can lead a heart-felt, thoughtful prayer with little or no preparation, many men cannot. By writing out their prayers prior to leading them, or at least outlining them, these men can think about the specific needs, struggles, joys, and challenges of a congregation and prepare to take these things to the throne of God in a very meaningful and inspiring way.

2) *Keep public prayers rather brief.* Although *brief* is a less than exacting term, this is as specific as I am willing to go with this suggestion. All I am trying to say is that when prayers go on and on and on, the attention and concentration of many people may begin to wane. Consequently, what may start out as a meaningful and inspirational prayer may end up less than inspiring. Prayer leaders need to be conscious of this danger and try to avoid leading *excessively* long prayers. I agree with those who suggest that it is better to have several short prayers in a public worship assembly than one excessively long prayer.

3) *Occasionally devote an entire service to prayer.* I am a firm believer that churches should conduct some sort of regular "prayer meeting." It may be once a month, once a quarter, or at some other regular interval, but prayer must occupy a place of primary importance in the life of God's people—individually *and* corporately.

In such a service different men may be called on to lead separate prayers on specific concerns, and these prayers may be interspersed with selected songs and readings from Scripture. Ideally, prayer assignments should be made far enough in advance to allow leaders adequate time to prepare what they will say to God on behalf of the church.

4) *Pray in a loud and clear voice.* This may sound elementary, but one of the greatest hindrances to a meaningful public prayer is the necessity of straining to hear the one who is leading the prayer. Prayer leaders need to remain conscious of this possible pitfall and speak loudly and clearly as they pray.

5) *Do away with memorized prayers.* This suggestion, like the first, is really about the need to put careful thought and preparation into prayer. We all probably know someone who leads virtually the same prayer, almost word for word, every time he prays publicly; and we all know how uninspiring and less than meaningful this can be. Memorized prayers smack of mere ritual, and we certainly do not want our worship to become a mere ritual.

Worship in Song

Most would probably agree that the quality of our "song service" does as much as anything in worship to determine whether or not our services are vibrant and meaningful or dull and lifeless. Dynamic singing can inspire people as nothing else can, while singing that comes across as indifferent and lifeless will lull them to sleep.

Here are some suggestions which have been offered to improve and enhance our efforts to worship God in song:

1) *Carefully select a song leader.* I believe the catalyst to a great song service is a great song leader. If this is true, church leaders need to assign the responsibility of leading God's people in singing only to those who possess the greatest talent, ability, desire, and technical competence.

Of course, some men have the natural gifts and desire to be good song leaders, while lacking the technical competence. In cases such as this, church leaders should be committed to helping such men become technically competent. How can they do this? Probably the most viable option for most churches is to hire an experienced, technically competent song leader to conduct a weekend training session for would-be song leaders.

2) *Select songs that are appropriate for the various activities in a service.* Some songs seem to be best suited for beginning or ending a period of worship. Others seem to be best suited for singing in connection with the Lord's Supper. Still others seem to be best suited as a lead-in to prayer or Scripture reading. As many have noted, if the content of a song does not seem to fit with what is happening in a service, it can be distracting to worshipers.

3) *Select more songs that have a vertical focus.* Since worship is primarily an occasion to ascribe honor and praise to God, songs that verbalize praise should be a central feature in our assemblies. I might add that songs with a strong vertical orientation will help a worshiper focus on God more than songs which are primarily horizontal in their orientation.

4) *Select appropriate songs for worship.* Not every song is appropriate for use in Christian worship. Appropriate songs for worship will have certain characteristics. One, they will reflect a basic theme or insight into Christian theology or the Christian experience. Two, they will be in harmony with Scripture. Three, they will not reflect an excessive emphasis on selfish concerns. Four, their rhythm will express the tone or the feelings of the lyrics. Five, they will contain clear and understandable language. And six, they will have a rhythm that is appropriate for entrance into the divine assembly.[2]

5) *Select songs that most worshipers know.* It can be frustrating, and certainly not very inspirational, when most of the congregation is unfamiliar with the songs which are selected for a worship service. Of course, this does not mean that churches should shun learning new songs. Churches should always be looking for new, appropriate songs to add to their repertoire. I am simply suggesting that the worship assembly—at least the primary Lord's day assembly—may not be the best time for learning new songs.

Personal Responsibility

It would be a mistake to hold church leaders fully responsible for making public worship vibrant and meaningful.

There are several things that only an individual worshiper can do to ensure that public worship is an enriching, meaningful, and inspirational experience. What are they?

For one thing, worshipers must spend time in private worship. If a person's private worship life is virtually non-existent, it will be virtually impossible to find meaning and inspiration in public worship. On the other hand, those who spend time regularly communing with God through private prayers, Scripture reading, and hymns of praise are much more likely to find meaning and inspiration when they gather with God's people to worship.

Another thing that worshipers can do to make worship more meaningful is to prepare themselves physically and mentally prior to worship. Speaking from personal experience, it is difficult to find enrichment in public worship if a person is physically exhausted or has not taken time to meditate on God and spiritual matters prior to a public service. If a person goes to bed late on Saturday night, wakes up late on Sunday morning, frantically rushes to get everyone in the house dressed and fed, speeds into the church parking lot one minute past time to begin, runs into the building carrying a child under each arm, and collapses into a pew tense, haggard, and exhausted, that person should almost *expect* to find the service minimally enriching.

Most people will find public worship much more meaningful and inspirational if they will get plenty of sleep on Saturday, rise early on Sunday, spend a few minutes in reflective reading from the Psalms or some other portion of Scripture, spend a few minutes in prayer, wake the family in time to dress, eat, and drive to the building at a casual pace, and arrive at the building several minutes prior to the scheduled start of a service.

Still another thing that worshipers can do to ensure that worship is as meaningful as it can be is to keep in mind the primary purpose of worship as they attend public services. Worshipers are more likely to find meaning, inspiration, and enrichment in public worship if they keep in mind that they are there primarily to give honor and praise to God, not to get some sort of personal reward. As was noted earlier, God has designed worship in such a way that its fullest blessings are bestowed on those who worship primarily in order to give rather than to get. Those who go to worship primarily seeking emotional gratification through entertainment, or some other personal payoff, will often find the service uninspiring or less than meaningful regardless of how effectively each element or activity is carried out.

Conclusion

Much more could be said on this subject, but hopefully enough has been said to provide a starting point for those seeking to make public worship more vibrant and meaningful while staying within the framework of Scripture, and without framing worship as entertainment. Also, hopefully enough has been said to convince people that meaningful, inspirational worship depends as much on individual worshipers as it does on church leaders.

Questions to Guide Study

1. What are some ways to enhance and improve our efforts around the Lord's table?

2. Do you think public Scripture reading should be a central feature of our assemblies? Why or why not?

3. What are some ways to enhance and improve our efforts to read Scripture publicly?

4. What are some ways to enhance and improve our corporate prayers?

5. When it comes to making worship vibrant and meaningful, how important do you think the "song service" is?

6. What are some ways to enhance and improve our efforts to worship God in song?

7. Do you think it is important to conduct each activity of our assemblies in the most effective way possible? Why or why not?

8. Do you think individual worshipers bear any responsibility for making public worship meaningful? Explain your answer.

Endnotes

[1] Two works that I found especially helpful in this area were Ted Waller's *Worship: Bowing at the Feet of God* (Nashville, TN: 20th Century Christian, 1994) and Dan Dozier's *Come Let Us Adore Him* (Joplin, MO: College Press, 1994). The fact that I strongly disagree with Dozier in areas such as hand raising does not diminsh the value of some his suggestions for making public worship as meaningful and inspirational as possible.

[2] For an expanded discussion of these charactristics, see Chapter 7, pages 105-107.